MW01616678

GASPING FOR
AIR

GASPING FOR
AIR

MY CHAOTIC JOURNEY THROUGH
DIAGNOSIS, DESPAIR, AND HOPE

SARA LAWLER SMITH

atmosphere press

© 2023 Sara Lawler Smith

Published by Atmosphere Press

Cover design by Kevin Stone

No part of this book may be reproduced without permission from the author except in brief quotations and in reviews.

Atmospherepress.com

This is dedicated to the amazing Dr. Rachel Kingree and incomparable Dr. Lisa Young; the two badass women who literally saved my life.

Twice.

I had the best dream recently, and I swear, it's not for the sake of the story. This was an actual dream and it felt realistic as hell.

I was running. Just running. Down some generic road. Breath visible in the cool air, trees lining the street, and the sounds of my feet hitting the pavement in a steady rhythm. The scenery isn't really important though; the running is.

Things were so simple in this dream. Even better? In this dream I was happy. Elated even.

You'll see why.

But goddamn. I think it is possibly the best dream I have ever had.

INTRODUCTION

Before we get to the sarcasm, the foul mouth, and the raw honesty surrounding everything that happened on and after December 2nd, 2014, there is one thing that you really need to know in the purest sense. With no humor, no poorly crafted defense mechanisms, and no shades of grey.

Grief. Is bullshit.

A very popular model has been used to visually represent the grief process.

Per that model, these are the five stages of grief:

- Denial

- Anger

- Depression

- Bargaining

- Acceptance

If you find yourself online, as we all do for more hours a day than we care to admit (especially with the introduction of TikTok), go ahead and Google a few images of the infamous Kubler-Ross grief model. Examples will depict the stages in a straight line, in a list, or as a cycle. No matter which image is shown, it's portrayed as a one-way street. A process with a defined start and finish that begins with denial and ends at acceptance. Only in the last few years have I discovered how truly misleading this model is.

I can only assume the model has morphed into this version because an accurate portrait of how the stages of grief *actually* play out would offer no comfort to anyone who may be using its premise as a mechanism for survival.

When one grieves in real time, the process is not linear. Not even a little bit. One does not benefit from the solace of knowing that once they have left denial, they will never have to return. Or that once they get past the anger, they will never be angry about whatever they are grieving in that moment ever again. Or even that, when they reach acceptance, they won't ever have to try and muddle through the previous four excruciating phases.

The real truth is, you spend some time in denial, then anger, then back to denial, then you fumble blindly into depression, then back to anger, until the cycle feels endless and you can barely make sense of which way is up or where you are in the process.

But I'm not here to talk about everyone else, as much as I would like to deflect just a little while longer. When it comes to my situation, I have yet to reach acceptance, even after all this time. I have spent the entirety of the years since everything that happened since December 2nd, 2014, navigating the highway between denial and anger without veering from the Mario Kart-like course and it's a bitch of a commute.

The manifestation of *my* personal grief process was two-fold. In addition to becoming an angry individual, a character trait that, in the past, had been intermittently present but never constant, I also spent the majority of my time navigating my way through an emotional breakdown. My days (sometimes hours) fluctuated between anger and sadness without any other emotions to even out my psyche. It was both physically and mentally exhausting.

I often wonder how people who have been angry their entire lives (and we have all met those people) hold jobs, have relationships, and/or build friendships. Even presently, there are times I still wouldn't be the least bit surprised to lose all three of those things in one fell swoop. And no one in my life at that time would be at fault if they simply flipped me the bird and said "fuck you, I'm out."

I was miserable 99.9% of that time. And what made it even worse, I didn't have the energy to fake happiness.

All that to say, even in my darkest moments, I could still rationalize at least some of the sadness; the depression; even the anxiety.

But, the anger?

It had no logic.

It followed no rules.

Nothing and no one were off limits. Nine times out of ten, my below the belt jabs were directed at someone who had done nothing but attempt to soften the blow for me. I have not yet reached a place where I am not angry, although that really is the dream.

I *have*, however, reached a place where I am able to suppress it (I know, extremely healthy) and not project it onto others. While I still have more moments than I care to admit where I boil over for no good reason (*that* book will be written by my husband), they seem to be more intermittent than before.

So, couple poor coping skills with a complete disbelief in anything to do with the great beyond, and you have me: a sarcastic meanderer with an endless number of defense mechanisms and an even higher tolerance for dark liquor.

This book is my attempt at catharsis. It is my attempt to cope. It is also my attempt at finding people like me. Not with my diagnosis necessarily, but with a general and overwhelming fear of believing no one out there knows exactly how you feel.

And maybe, while I wish upon a star, this will help propel

me to a place where I can achieve what I have craved since all of this started. The end of the winding and unknown path that is grief.

Perhaps, this will get me there. To acceptance.

And while I desire many things—love, pizza, being thin, and being thin because I only eat pizza—I have wanted nothing more over these past years than reaching acceptance; because maybe with acceptance, comes the exhale.

CHAPTER ONE

The Beginning
December 2nd, 2014

I walked into work on December 2nd, 2014, like I would have on any other Tuesday; glad Monday was over, but feeling as if the upcoming Friday was too far in the distance to provide me any solace, let alone any insight on how quickly my work week would come to an end. I had smoked my ritual three Marlboro Menthol Lights on the way to work and was already craving another.

My overwhelming phobia of the Nashville interstate (likely a result of my small-town upbringing) had landed me a nursing job that was not in a hospital and more importantly, a job where I could hire and train my own staff, and one where my commute allowed me to steer clear of Interstate 40; a 4-lane dumpster fire of a highway. While I was still not entirely convinced office life was for me; the conviviality and friendships had proven to work in my favor.

As I always did upon arrival, I meandered around the department looking for someone to engage in small talk with before I had to address the inane contents of my always overflowing email inbox. One of the nurses I'd recently hired (who had also become a friend rather rapidly) had already arrived for the day. I was grateful for the ten- to fifteen-minute distraction that would ensue as a result of us arriving before upper level management.

I made my way over to her desk to commune with her and the few other staff members who were also early birds. I sat on the edge of a desk, discussing some unimportant piece of gossip or random insurance review we were working on and, literally out of nowhere, I felt a sharp twinge of pain in my chest.

It alarmed me, albeit briefly. I was only thirty-two, after all, but a pretty regular smoker and an excessive coffee drinker. But still, there was definitely just a fleeting "something" that caused me a moment of pause and the hope that the three cups of coffee that I had already consumed even before I left the house had not started eating away at my esophagus.

"Well, that was oddly uncomfortable," I said, while I sipped on coffee number four.

"Everything okay?" someone said.

I nodded and continued to sip.

Then, almost as quickly as the pain had manifested, it was nearly gone. As a precaution, or more likely out of habit, I walked back to my desk and popped four Ibuprofen. Chest pain was going to do nothing more than annoy me today, even if it was just a miniscule level of pain. As I washed the pills down with my black coffee, there was one final moment, as my mind wandered for a second or two, when I wondered if I had a blood clot—a self-diagnosis that any good nurse would have given themselves. I let the thought linger briefly before writing it off as an idiotic idea.

You're fine, I said to myself as I took a seat at my desk.

Just as I knew it would, the pain eventually subsided completely and my normal Tuesday was back in full swing. A morning that would be spent listening to Billy Joel on my iPod while combing through my emails. What I didn't know then, as I sat staring at my computer screen, was that day would become the most life-altering day I would ever experience. I look back on it now and wish I had known what was coming; wish I'd had a chance to prepare. I'm not 100% sure that would have changed anything, but it still would have been nice to brace myself for the impact.

By 9:00 a.m., I was sitting in a meeting that had nothing to do with nursing (another downside to nurses working in an office that employees primarily non-medical staff) and everything to do with "percent of revenue," "high dollar write-offs," and a bunch of other financial jargon that I'm sure was important but made me want to shove cotton balls in my ears.

As I attempted to focus, I was overcome with the sudden urge to cough each time I took a breath. For the second time that day, just for a second, I had a feeling that maybe there really was something wrong.

"You don't look good," someone said from somewhere that sounded oddly far away.

Rude, I thought.

Instead of being insulted, I *should* have been nervous.

"Eh, it's probably just a clot," I said. I only half meant it; mostly I just wanted to stop talking about my health in a room full of people on a seemingly normal Tuesday morning. I silently wondered how many cups of coffee was too many and contemplated leaving campus for lunch, which I rarely did. Maybe all I needed was some fresh air and a plate of mozzarella sticks from the Applebee's down the road.

The meeting finished (not a second too soon) and I headed down the hall to my desk. I had only been walking for a few seconds when I felt the immediate need to sit down and inhale all of the air around me, as if I was about to submerge myself under water for an extended period of time.

I took a beat and then continued to saunter down the hall, almost in a fugue, willing my body to make it back to my desk without incident. At some point, as I participated in the longest walk of all time, I felt a hand on my shoulder. My new hire and

9

even newer friend was standing just behind me, and I could tell by the look on her face that she felt like something was off.

"Let's check your O2, just to be safe." Her tone informed me that this was very clearly not a request. "I have a portable O2 monitor in my purse. Throw it on and we'll just go for a quick walk."

Of course she did. While I felt like checking my oxygen level as I walked up and down the breakroom hall was a gross over-reaction, I did not have the energy to argue. Sure, I felt "weird" but my body was likely just rejecting the insane amounts of nicotine and caffeine I had ingested before 10:00 a.m. I be-grudgingly agreed, mostly so she would shut up about it. I had not known my new hire that long, but I knew her well enough to know I was going to do what she said or I would never hear the end of it.

We walked slowly up and down the hall, as if I was walk-ing the Green Mile, and as much as I tried, I couldn't shake that cloudy feeling. I pushed down each cough that attempted to escape with each breath, thinking that as long as I could do that, I'd be fine and we could go back to our desks and forget this was even a thing.

"Well," she said as we took our last lap, "your heart rate is up and your O2 went down." There it was again; a brief but very obvious look of concern. "I think we should take you to the hospital. Just to be safe."

I didn't have time to go to the hospital. Hell, I didn't have time to be pacing the halls with an O2 monitor dangling from my finger.

"We can, but I just need to check some emails and..."

I didn't even get a chance to finish my sentence. She shot me a look that said "I don't want to hear it" and I gave in. I was going to make her feel like a real shit when the hospital sent me home with a clean bill of health. We let our manager know we'd be leaving and ten minutes later, we were driving down the interstate toward the nearest hospital. There was no doubt I felt a little off, but I was not nearly as concerned as she seemed to be. Some '90s pop song came on the radio and I instinctively began performing at a concert level.

"Stop singing along to this song. You already can't breathe."

I made a comment about her being far too worried about me and, as a fellow vocal performance major, she of all people should have known you *never* tell a singer not to sing. And while singing along to the radio was a far cry from all of the stages I had been on, it was the only time I got to sing since my move to Nashville. She, however, seemed unphased by the statement and instead of allowing me to finish my aria, she promptly turned off the radio.

We arrived at the ER shortly before 11:00 a.m. The hospital sat at the top of a small hill and, while I was indeed out of shape, the walk to the main entrance seemed particularly daunting that morning. By the time I reached the lobby, I could barely catch my breath.

And there it was again. That fleeting fear—but it held on just a bit longer this time.

I was snapped out of my moment of dread by a gruff man who I am convinced was an actual hobgoblin, and he seemed quite annoyed that I couldn't breathe well enough to answer his ridiculous litany of questions. As he took the last of my information, he made some snide comment after my inability to inhale oxygen caused me to miss some tidbit of information. I made a mental note to add him to my "list" and subsequently took a seat in the mostly empty waiting room.

It wasn't too long before I was called back to the triage room and, as the nurse completed her workup, I felt a wave of embarrassment come over me. Everything was normal. Blood pressure, oxygen, heartrate, EKG. Not one result was concerning or unusual. I sat there mortified and could feel my face get hot while I listened to the nurse tell me we were just waiting on my blood work.

Great, I thought. *I'll look even crazier when all of those numbers are normal as well.*

As I sat in the small room waiting for my results, I heard the door open and an ER doctor walked in. It's odd for an ER doctor to meet you in triage, but I thought nothing of it. Perhaps he was going to lecture me on the importance of utilizing an Urgent Care instead of an ER for non-life threatening situations.

I cringed as he walked into the room, result in hand, and I had never been more thankful that I had not disclosed my profession. I could just picture him at the dinner table with his family, mocking the nurse who "thought she was dying for no damn reason."

"Well, your D-dimer..."

(a blood test they use to check for the presence of a clot)

"...is elevated, which means you probably have a clot."

Well, shit.

My new friend and I stole a quick glance as he explained the meaning of the blood work and how I would be getting a CT scan, and what that entailed, and...

As I half listened to a test I knew all about, I felt a wave of relief. It sounds strange, I know, considering I was clearly having an acute medical issue, but at least I didn't have to leave with my tail between my legs and a judgey look from the monster at the front desk. Looks like this was going to be an easy fix, just a quick shot of a blood thinner after my CT and I'd be on my way. Maybe I would even luck out and get to be out of work for a few days. It had been a while since I'd had the time to binge watch *Hoarders* and *My 600-lb. Life.*

"Can you text Dan and tell him everything is okay?" I asked, suddenly remembering that the boyfriend I had moved to Nashville for in the first place had no clue I was even in the emergency room.

A nod.

He was one of the most anxious people I'd ever met and would have worried for no reason. The words "I'm going to the ER" were enough to send him into a full panic since, even on normal days, he was wound tighter than a piano string. Sadly, since I was not going to be leaving with a clean bill of health, the call had to be made.

It's a strange thing to say, but I quite fondly remember the window of time between my trip to radiology and my meeting with the physician to talk about my CT results. It was a time where I had no thoughts of anything other than what I was going to have for dinner that night or if Dan would use this "terrifying" event as a sign he should propose. We had our answer, I knew the treatment, and the strangeness of the day was nearing an end.

Unfortunately, the strangeness had only just begun and it would be far too long before my thought allowed me to even have a moment's peace. Somewhere, amidst the calm and seemingly out of nowhere, my room was suddenly flooded with nurses, multiple doctors, all speaking to each other and glancing in my direction every so often.

How long had they been talking? What was I missing? Had they been in the room for a while? What in hell was happening?

"...noticed some abnormalities on your CT..."

"...pneumothorax..."

(Fancy talk for collapsed lung.)

I had a collapsed lung? At least that's what I think they were telling me. It was taking me a minute to focus.

"...do you know what a pneumothorax is?"

Yes, I'm a nurse.

Shit. Did I say that out loud, or did I just think it?

If I had said anything aloud, it didn't much matter. The doctor continued to talk, and he had already begun to tell me that they were contacting the pulmonologist on call and she would be there to answer any questions....

...*should* I have questions?...

...and to please let the staff know if there was anything at all I needed.

I'll say this. There is one thing that the TV medical dramas get right. The worse the news, the more people in the room when it's delivered. I was suddenly glaringly aware of the increasing number of medical staff that were in the room with me and just like that, the fear was back and, despite my attempt at pushing it out of my mind, this time it was lingering.

Relax, I told myself. *Take a deep breath*. Oh wait, you can't.

Instead, I closed my eyes and attempted to drown out all of the noise. After what felt like barely a moment, I heard all of the voices stop and opened my eyes to see a new doctor in the room.

My pulmonologist was probably the most adorable human being I'd ever met. In any other circumstance, I would have turned to whoever was standing next to me and made some sarcastic comment comparing her to Doogie Howser, because of both her young looks and sandy blonde hair. Instead, as she entered the room, she brought a calmness in with her and I felt safe.

Without missing a beat, she introduced herself and then began to talk about my scan. She made some vague references to emphysema (deserved) and COPD (also not a surprise). I was young but I was also a smoker. Shitty news? Sure. Abnormal for someone my age? Yes. But nothing unheard of. She wasn't done, however, and the last thing she did was spout out some long, fancy, doctor-y diagnosis that I'd never heard of. Not even in passing. I brushed that last thing off even before she had finished saying it.

Nursing school 101: If you hear hoofbeats behind you,
think horse **NOT** zebra.

My brain did not need to waste time and energy processing some super-rare disease that sounded like a sneeze when it was said out loud. Especially since the odds of having it were (as I later found out) literally one in a million. I was certainly not at a point of no fear like I had been at the start of this insane and random day, but I was far from consistent thoughts of impending doom.

Besides, most lung collapses are spontaneous and never happen again. I was having a random medical occurrence that would end with some pain meds and a great story to tell over cocktails that weekend.

"We are going to have to insert a chest tube to reinflate your lung," the doctor said. "It's going to feel like a big splinter." I could tell it was a line she had said many times before, and yet, there was nothing in her tone that felt rehearsed. "Morphine is available if you feel like you need it."

I shook my head "no." I would love to pretend like it was the nurse in me who wanted to turn down an opiate, but it was 100% my ego speaking for me. And seriously. How much can a tiny little tube hurt?

The procedure itself happened quickly and with no pain.

Giant splinter? I thought. *People will complain about anything.*

What seemed like the exact moment she finished completing the stitch to hold the tube in place, I was quickly wheeled out of the room for another x-ray. She made some mention of making sure my tube was placed in the right spot, but I was only half paying attention; the exhaustion of the day had finally sunk in and I could not wait to get to a room, any room, and sleep.

As I arrived (for the second time) in the familiar radiology suite, the tech looked at me and, with an almost pained tone, said, "We are going to have to roll you on your side."

She quickly turned away, and I wondered why she was talking to me like being rolled like a beached whale was going to be the worst part of my day.

I was about to find out.

I have a pretty high tolerance for pain. Not to say I don't

feel pain or that I'm one of those people who *enjoys* it, but I'll cry quicker at a Hallmark movie than I will because something hurts.

As she rolled me on my side, the level of pain I felt was indescribable. The tears came swiftly and without warning, along with an audible yelp.

Giant splinter, my ass.

My involuntary vocal response obviously rattled the radiology technician; she took the x-rays with swiftness I've never seen and without saying another word, whisked me back to the room I had now been occupying for several hours.

Apparently, somewhere during the procedure I had started to cry, and I was still crying when I got back to my "suite." The tears were impossible to stop. Everything happening around me seemed blurred by the pain and I was unable to focus on anything else. I needed someone to do something to make it go away.

Without verbal prompting (but using my tears as a green light), my friend pressed the call bell next to my head, and a nurse quickly entered my room. She returned not long after with a shot that I could only hope was a horse tranquilizer of some sort.

Morphine is a funny thing. It's not like other pain medications where you wait fifteen minutes and the pain goes away or at least decreases somewhat. You are most definitely still in pain as the liquid flows through your veins. You just don't fucking care. Once the medicine hit my system, I didn't care about the pain, the collapsed lung, or the laundry list of things the pulmonologist said could possibly be wrong with me. I just cared that I was on morphine. And it was glorious.

Somewhere between the chest tube and the morphine, Dan had arrived. He sat in the corner of the room and would look up from his phone every once in a while with a reassuring smile. If he was annoyed, or scared, or tired, he never let on. I felt like a real shit for putting him through all of this; newly dating after years of a "will they, won't they" on a Ross and Rachel level, and I was already bringing the drama.

Eventually, my room was acquired and I was able to finally leave the ER. I couldn't wait to get to a place that was a bit quieter, take a deep breath, and attempt to digest the events of the day. The morphine had worn off and the pain was back, just in time for me to send everyone home.

"Finally," I said to no one.

Alone with my thoughts, I went through the events of the day over and over again.

Could it be COPD? Emphysema? The random life-threatening lung disease?

No. I pushed those thoughts away and silently recited a mantra.

Spontaneous pneumothorax.

It happens all the time.

This is most likely nothing.

Somehow, my nurse worst-case-scenario brain eventually shut off for the night and I attempted to get some sleep. While I had moments of comfort that would allow me to drift off, I would quickly be interrupted by a stabbing pain that occurred anytime I so much as blinked. Sleep was not going to come. At least not a sound one, so I turned on the TV, found a *Dateline* marathon, and drifted in and out of consciousness to the voice of Keith Morrison.

That was the last night I would spend not thinking about my life in a completely different way; not thinking about why I got dealt the cards I did; not thinking about dying. After that night, every day would be a battle between me and my brain; me telling my brain to shut the hell up and my brain politely telling me to fuck off.

CHAPTER TWO

The Next Day
December 3rd, 2014

When I was eighteen and a freshman in college, my friend died in a car accident about two weeks before Christmas. The days that immediately followed were hazy and I felt as if I was living in some strange state between sleep and fully awake.

That is what my life was like every day for the month (or two...or ten...) after December 2nd, 2014.

In retrospect (and due to my experience as a nurse who specialized in mental illness), it should have been a tad clearer to me what I was experiencing.

The death of my health. And the death of my life as I knew it.

Perhaps my lack of clarity was due to the fact that I was still blissfully unaware of the true severity of my illness. Or maybe it was because I was in the midst of a crisis and had little to no clarity. Or maybe, I was in denial. (Fucking duh.)

Whatever the reason (it was denial), I was unable to step away from the moment and view things on a larger scale. I couldn't acknowledge that this was going to be a process. That with any death—be it death in the sense of losing a loved one or just the death of a part of your life that was lost—comes grief.

And with all grief comes the infamous five stages. Or steps. Or cyclical hellscape that never ends. Six of one, half dozen of the other.

Do I think knowing this would have offered me solace at the time?

Most likely not. It's probable that ignorance was my best defense mechanism. And still is. But a heads-up would have been nice. "Hey, this is going to be awful. So, buckle up."

All of those thoughts and feelings were looming on the horizon, and I should have relished the solace that came with my ignorance. I still believed I had experienced a random, albeit horribly ill-timed lung collapse. I told myself I would be out of the hospital in a day or two and this would all be some crazy story I could tell like the time I ordered pizza and had to get stitches. (What did I tell you? Accident-prone as hell.)

So, instead of worrying, I lay in the hospital bed the night before and well into the morning still blissfully unaware of the shitstorm that was headed my way. That being said, it was still quite far from a comfortable night and I slept like absolute shit.

It was my first time sleeping in a hospital, and periods of wake and sleep were intermixed with continued pain and routine nurse checks. I can say with confidence it was probably the worst night's sleep I'd ever had, with the exception of the summer I had mono.

Let's talk about the pain for a second. Because holy fuck. There is pain, and then there is chest-tube pain. What they don't tell you is that with a chest tube, not only does it feel like a dull blade is constantly scooping out your insides, but also that no matter what you do, how you move or don't move, that pain will never go away. And that every time you cough, sneeze, laugh, cry, or do a Kegel, the tube that has been placed in that space hits one of the thousands of nerves that are between your lungs and rib cage.

And go ahead. Take all the pain medications you want; there is never any relief, although I imagine a medically induced coma, or death, could have done the trick. So, between that, and the constant swarm of medical staff who seemed to be able to predict with scary accuracy what time I would doze off, I may have gotten about two or three hours of sleep.

I was not the most pleasant person in the world the following morning. Frankly, I was likely in the running for being the biggest bitch in the state at that point. Despite my less than chipper demeanor, Dan sat silently by my side. Normally, he was the king of positivity manor, but today, his mind seemed otherwise occupied. Maybe he already knew my fate; I've never asked.

They say nurses make the worst patients. Well, give that nurse a chest tube and that takes things to a whole new level. I was already tired, pissed, and ready to punch a baby square in the face. So, when the sweetest doctor I'd ever met came into my room, and she wasn't smiling, the little positivity I had left was shot to shit. I silently cursed myself for all those years I'd smoked and promised the God I didn't believe in that I would never have another cigarette.

Emphysema. In my thirties. Winning at life.

But it wasn't emphysema.

Or COPD.

Or asthma.

Or a random Tuesday lung collapse that would happen once and never again.

The kind doctor pulled up a chair and sat next to me; an obvious communication tactic used in an attempt to make me feel more comfortable and that she was empathizing. She tried to smile but I could tell that it was forced; something she felt like she had to do to soften the blow of what was about to happen and maybe ease the palpable tension.

It wasn't working. I was legitimately petrified.

Dan grabbed my hand; odd, I could almost tell it was out

of fear as opposed to habit.

"I got on Google last night..."

Her voice immediately trailed off and my brain was set on fire. Google. My doctor was using Google. There was no way in hell whatever happened after this was going to be in my favor.

I was right.

"You have lymphangioleiomyomatosis."

I'm sorry, say what now? Apparently, we were in the stage of the game where we were just making up words. This must have been that long and random word I had heard several times the day before and brushed off as an impossibility.

As I got a crash course on lymphangioleiomyomatosis (or LAM for the sake of time), she went on to tell me that my lungs were filled with tiny cysts that were multiplying and eating away at my healthy lung tissue. This would continue until I did not have enough healthy lung tissue to circulate air and I would either need a transplant or...she didn't say 'die' out loud, but her face certainly said it.

Dan squeezed my hand tighter and tighter and she told us she was unsure of the etiology, or the prognosis, or how far progressed it was, or anything helpful for that matter. She apologized, promised she would continue to research, tried to smile, and left the room to give me "time to process." I somehow managed to wait until she left the room before I burst into tears.

Horse, my ass, I thought. *This is the definition of a mother fucking zebra.*

I looked over at Dan, hoping to get a read on the situation. Maybe it wasn't as bad as I thought. As anxious as he was most times, he was also an eternal optimist. For the first time in the year and a half we had been dating, I couldn't read his face, which did nothing to squash the overwhelming feeling of mortality that had washed over me. I attempted to calm myself down.

You're overreacting.

You need to calm down.
Just breathe.
You can't breathe.
Your lungs are shot.
You can't handle this.
Crying will fix everything.
You're going to die.
Good job, brain. Seriously. Well fucking done.

I had to get it together. I needed to be somewhere else, and alone to process everything that had just happened. All of the things I had just been told. That was not going to happen if I couldn't open my mouth without crying or yelling expletives.

Eventually, I was able to "self-tranquilize" myself enough to inform the staff that I wanted to go home. The kind doctor entered my room one last time and agreed (or more likely felt so guilty about the news that she would have done anything I asked) that I could be discharged. My lung seemed to have begun behaving and, as a result, I could have the medieval torture device removed from my chest cavity and thrown into the garbage where it belonged.

Had I known what this next part entailed, I would likely still be lying in that hospital bed trying to work up the courage to give the doctor the go-ahead.

I try not to swear in public. Shocking, I know. I usually save my exquisitely placed profanities for the safety of my own home. Or a bar. Or in traffic. Or on a Tuesday. Okay, so maybe saying I don't swear in public is a bit of a stretch.

Let me try again. I usually don't swear in front of people I don't know very well. So, while I do enjoy profanity with a purpose, I am always very aware of the fact that it's coming out of my mouth.

The string of swear words that occurred as the doctor pulled the tube out of my chest was nothing short of breathtaking. (Get it?) And it certainly was not planned, although it was quite exquisite as far as improvisational swearing is concerned.

"Fuckingsonofabitchmotherfuckingshittyshitfucker."

Not exact, but close.

The doctor laughed nervously while Dan looked like he wanted to disown me. I could have given two shits about anyone or anything at that moment. The tube was out. The pain was over. All I wanted to do was get out of the hospital, get on my laptop, and Google until my fingers bled. If the doctor could do it, so could I.

I had to know everything.

CHAPTER THREE

The Aftermath
December 2014 and January 2015

I left the hospital on December 3rd with too many questions to count and no one to ask.

The first week home, time seemed to move at a snail's pace. Dan and I had only moved in together a few months prior and I thought my time would be filled with a lot more sex and a lot less planning my own funeral. Work had given me time off "indefinitely," likely so I could cope with my impending and suddenly much closer to the present death. Dan was gone all day and, as a result, I was left with nothing but an idle mind and plenty of time to throw myself down any rabbit hole I could find. And there were plenty to choose from.

My funeral.

A lung transplant.

My singing. God, was I going to lose the ability to sing?

When I wasn't overthinking, my time included making sure I thanked everyone who brought food, flowers, or well-wishes, the occasional booze-induced breakdown, and endless hours online trying to figure out how many years I had left to live (five to ten years after diagnosis from what I could gather). I spent almost all of the time I was awake hunched over my tiny laptop attempting to make some semblance of sense out of the diagnosis I'd been given.

After week one, my typical day was split up into three parts. A good cry in the morning, multiple naps in the afternoon, and "look up your diagnosis until you are so exhausted from your imminent death that you pass out" in the evening. Then I would wake up and do it all over again. I fielded texts and phone calls the only way I knew how: by completely ignoring them.

On the rare occasion I did answer the phone, the conversation was brief. Due to my rigorous schedule of daily breakdowns, I only had the mental capacity to lie once per phone call. As a result, they usually went something like this:

Them: "How are you?"

Me: "Oh, I'm fine."

Them: "Are you sure?"

Me: "Yes, I'm sure."

Them: "*Really?*" (Obvious disbelief.)

Me: "I have to go."

I usually hung up before they could ask me one more time if I was "really, really, okay."

As far as my Google searches, the information seemed to be sparse at best. And yet, each day I got online and read the same information over and over. I would read and reread, cry myself into a nap, and wake up just to do the same thing again; mindlessly scrolling through the ten-ish websites I found that had any sort of information. Here is both a boring and extremely macabre compilation of the non-evidence-based medical information I read and reread every single day for three weeks.

This information kept me in a constant state of being mid-panic. (*Please note: The words listed in bold are the only portions of data my brain felt was relevant to retain.*)

WebMD:

Pulmonary lymphangioleiomyomatosis is progressive, and so far, there is no cure. Most women with LAM experience a steady decline in lung function, with increased shortness of breath over time.

However, women vary widely in their experience of living with LAM lung disease. Some rapidly progress while others progress slowly: in some studies, nearly 90% of women were alive 10 years after diagnosis with LAM. **However, surviving as long as 20 years after diagnosis is rare.**

Medscape:

<u>Prognosis</u> *(So glad the websites were including this portion so I could dive right into the spiral.)*

Earlier reports indicated a grim prognosis for lymphangioleiomyomatosis (LAM), with progressive respiratory failure and death within 10 years of diagnosis. *Recent reports, however, are more favorable, with 71% of affected patients alive at 10 years. [8] The statistics may improve further as patients are diagnosed earlier (lead-time bias) or with more benign disease.*

Poor prognostic factors include the following:

Reduced forced expiratory volume in one second and/ or diffusing capacity for carbon monoxide.

A low LAM histology score, which quantifies the involvement of the lung with both LAM cells and cysts.

Merck Manuals:

Prognosis is unclear because the disorder is so rare *and because the clinical course of patients with LAM is* *variable. In general, the disease is slowly progressive, leading eventually to respiratory failure and death, but the time to death varies widely among reports. Median survival is likely > 8 yr. from diagnosis.* **Lung function declines 2 to 3 times faster than it does in healthy people.** *Women should be advised that progression may accelerate during pregnancy.*

Treatment is **Sirolimus** *or* **Lung Transplantation.**

My mind had apparently decided that the best course of action was to take bits and pieces of everything I had read to form its own "worst-case scenario" conclusion. After all of my reading, I was convinced I was not going to live past fifty—and that seemed to be the best-case scenario. And not only was I going to die, but I was going to suffocate to death.

A singer. Losing her ability to breathe.

How Shakespearean.

If I wasn't an atheist, I would have been cursing every God prayed to by every religion in the world. I had nothing but time on my hands and surely could have addressed each of the three thousand plus Gods individually. But, due to my self-in-flicted lack of belief, I had no one to blame for my diagnosis, prognosis, or any other "-osis" I was experiencing. That made this already gigantic pill even harder to swallow.

Oh, shit. Did I forget to mention that? The atheism part?

My bad. Let's dive headfirst into that pool of acid for a minute. Seems like a fun and nonchalant way to take a break from talking about using Google to predict my death.

There are a lot of reasons I don't want to bring up my athe-ism; however, it's mostly because I know people will judge me; and I need people to like me. Yes. I *need* people to like me. And I'm fine with that. I know from experience that people tend to make assumptions when they find out you are an atheist; about your ideals, your personality, even the way you live your life. Ninety percent of the time I tell people I am a non-believer, they briefly look at me like I just shot their puppy; then I get looked at like I'm pitiful.

I don't want to feel pitiful.

And I want to be liked.

I want to be more than my beliefs or lack thereof; that's not realistic in the least. People's beliefs are part of their personality and my atheism is a part of mine and, as a result, it's a part of all of this, in a very major way. I'm not sure if I even realized that when everything first started going to hell, but I certainly realize it now.

To be clear, it was not my diagnosis that led me to atheism. In fact, it happened long before a chronic illness was even in my periphery. While I don't think I had completely written off God because of a single event, I am sure the sudden death of a friend when I was eighteen eventually led me down the path of wavering faith and ultimate, albeit unwanted, disbelief.

While I continue to struggle with my own ideals and how atheism affects my life and relationships, I do know one thing: my lack of belief was not a result of choice, but a result of circumstance. The wick was lit, for one reason or another, and then burned slowly until it was eventually extinguished. I literally had faith until I didn't. I am not sure if it happened that abruptly, but my recollection is that it did.

Can I be sure that atheism was part of the reason I have continued to grapple with having a healthy handle on life's circumstances?

No.

But do I think that it played a role?

Absolutely, I do.

So, there I was; too much Google, too many tears. And not enough God, it would seem.

A recipe for complete and utter disaster; and that was a best-case scenario.

CHAPTER FOUR

The Family

Somewhere in all of the mess, I had found the time (and the courage) to break the news to my family about my diagnosis. I'm sure that I (or Dan) told my mother while it was all happening but, for everyone else, it was likely after the first round of Internet searching and was less informative and more about me hyperventilating into the phone.

After crying fit number two-hundred and seventy-three, my mom and sister decided it was best for me to be around them for the holidays. My mother called about one week before Christmas to let me know the two of them, plus my sister's fiancé, were coming to town. I really just wanted to continue to be alone. I wanted to wallow by myself through the holidays like the heroine in the opening sequence of a Lifetime movie.

The conversation was different than our norm; usually we laughed, swore, and gossiped. I mean, this was the same woman who once told me if I didn't get my shit together and get a job, she would put a red light on the porch and rent me out. (She was mostly kidding.) Only rarely did our daily talks have a serious tone and, when they did, it was because one or both of us was trying to keep our emotions in check.

"We are coming to Nashville," she said, matter-of-factly.

Since it really wasn't a question, I didn't get to answer with a resounding "no." The call was strictly informative, but I tried my best to deter the visit.

"We'll be there next week," my mother stated. Again, very clearly—not a question.

"You really don't have to come," I said. I meant it. I wanted to plead with her, beg her to leave me alone. But I couldn't get the words out.

"I know that, but we want to."

I didn't have the heart to tell her they would be better off staying home and celebrating with people who were much more likely to be the level of jolly required for the most wonderful time of the year.

"Just because of the diagnosis? That's dark, Mom." I forced out a quiet laugh so maybe she would think I was kidding. (I was not.)

"No, not just because of that," she said. She was obviously lying. "We're coming."

"Okay."

I knew I should have just grown a pair and told them not to come. I should have been honest and said that their presence was just a reminder that something was wrong. Horribly wrong even. And that the last thing I wanted to do was celebrate anything. Unfortunately (or maybe surprisingly is a more appropriate word), it seemed I did not have it in me to be that much of a bitch. As down as I was, I still had the wherewithal to know that the trip was more for their peace of mind than it was for mine.

Instead, I had just said okay and quickly hung up.

My mother had seemed relieved; I could tell even over the phone. It was almost as if she had been inside my head and knew I wanted to say no. Dan tried his best to get me excited about their impending visit. I wanted to feign excitement for his sake; especially since I knew he was also having to navigate his new normal as well.

"I know you'll be happy when they get here," he said a few days before their arrival.

"Will I?" I hadn't meant to say it out loud, but I didn't regret it.

For once, I was not being facetious, I really wanted to know. It had been such a dark and trying couple of weeks since my diagnosis that I wasn't 100% convinced anything could pull me out my funk.

He smiled, kissed my neck in the way that still made me melt, and nodded.

I so wanted him to be right, but I doubted it.

Remember when you were a kid, and there was something you weren't supposed to say to a specific person? And if you were going to see that person, your parents would sit you down and make sure you knew how important it was that you didn't say a word to that person about that thing? And do you remember how badly you just wanted to blurt it out?

Picture that moment for an entire week. That's how I felt for all of Christmas 2014.

We exclusively ate desserts and carbohydrates, watched movies (comedies only, of course) and discussed plans for my sister's upcoming wedding. Everything was normal except that it wasn't; it was almost like attending a weeklong wake that was only broken up by '90s romantic comedies and periodic ingestion of pasta and brownies.

Everyone was using all of their energy to come up with cheerful topics to discuss in the hopes of distracting me from the giant, wheezing elephant in the middle of the room. And other than the remnants of pain from the site of the chest tube placement, I didn't "feel sick." My breathing was normal, my energy was fine, and the only medical diagnosis that may have been slightly evident was my depression.

A day or two before Christmas dinner, I found myself and my mother alone.

"So..." she said.

Here it comes.

"How are you? Really."

A simple "fine" was not going to cut it with her.

"Well..." I said, trying to thinking about what I could say to end this conversation as quickly as possible. "It's a lot. I'm still digesting it all, I guess."

"I know." She was making her 'trying not to cry face.' I knew it well. "If you need anything...I just...I love you."

I told her I loved her too and swiftly grabbed the remote.

"Wanna watch something?"

She nodded and knew that meant I was done talking about it.

The first instance of a post-diagnosis happy moment happened on Christmas. I often wonder if my brother-in-law still thinks of it because, in any other instance, it was just our normal banter.

I decided to make a simple recipe for dinner. It was literally just lasagnas rolled into individual servings instead of one big lasagna. Frankly, it was all the effort I could muster. I cooked in the kitchen with the company of my sister and mother, while Dan and my sister's fiancé played video games in the next room.

Once the table was set and the spread was laid out on the random dresser that had taken residence in our kitchen, I called them in for dinner.

My sister's fiancé walked into the room, looked at our "fancy spread" and, in what can only be described as his best attempt at a British accent, said what would turn out to be the best words I'd heard in weeks.

"Oh, how fancy. We're having lasagna rolls," he said in a horrible British accent. Then, a grin slowly crept onto his face.

Without even thinking about it, I laughed. Hard. I didn't remember what laughing felt like. And, it was far from the funniest thing I had ever heard. But the universe knew I needed to feel something other than what I had been feeling.

That was the last time I laughed during their visit, because of all the serious stuff that still lingered, even after that brief moment of reprieve. Sometimes I would catch my mom or sister whispering to Dan in the next room, undoubtably to see if they would tell him how I really was. Occasionally, I would pop my head in the room and say, "I'm good, I promise." Most of the time, I would let them talk amongst themselves. While I was in my own head a lot of the time, I was not so oblivious that I didn't know they weren't all going through something as well.

Of course, now I understand why they made that trip. They didn't want to be near me for me; not totally, anyway. It was for them. Proximity made the news easier to ingest. Even if we spent the holiday pretending to be blissfully unaware of the circumstances, the trip was dripping with fear of the unknown.

After Christmas, I spent the time between my initial lung collapse and my appointment wondering what would happen next. Was there still a chance I was misdiagnosed and this was all a big misunderstanding? Could it be possible that even with LAM, I would be free from any side effects or lung issues? Attempting to learn from my previous mistakes, I tried my best to stay off of the Internet, which proved extremely difficult for my idle mind. Since I had been granted time off of work to "process everything," I had nothing to do but sit alone in my own thoughts.

While I still spent a considerable amount of time online because I'm not only dramatic but also a glutton for the melancholy, I filled the remaining hours of each day with Netflix, naps, and beer; all in an attempt to keep my mind lubricated to the point of amnesia. I don't remember if it worked or not—I just remember feeling as if I was living in the land where time stood still. Somehow, I made it through and got to my appointment day. I wouldn't call it excitement that I was feeling, but anticipation. Answers, even bad ones, had to be better than this constant state of pulmonary purgatory.

After about three weeks off, I decided to go back to work. I was told that I could stay out as long as I needed and, in hindsight, I wonder if that was for my benefit, that of my colleagues, or both. If the roles were reversed, I'm not sure I would know what to say to someone who left one day and came back to work actively dying.

I had to go back though. It was time. As healthy as it was to live off of pasta and self-loathing, I knew I had to get back into some semblance of a routine. More importantly, I was curious to see if I could make it through an entire day without crying in a bathroom stall.

Walking into work that first day was awful. And the reason I thought it was awful is going to make me sound even more awful. But fuck, I was not mentally prepared for a bunch of people trying to ask me questions while doing their best to sound like it was just a casual inquiry.

Everyone wanted to know how I was.

How I had been.

What they could do.

And the people who didn't ask just looked at me with the equivalent of the "you're an atheist pity eyes."

I answered all the questions as succinctly as possible and scurried over to my cubicle.

My friend—who I'm still convinced saved my life that day—arrived almost at the same time and took up residence with a seat on my desk.

Shit. Angie. Her name is Angie. She's in this a bunch, so let's give her a name, shall we?

"Well?"

It wasn't until she asked the question that I realized I really hadn't talked to her since everything happened. Maybe a text here or there to let her know I was "fine" but I really had buried myself in my thoughts with no concept of anything or anyone else. Since I had only talked through this with myself, I didn't quite know how to respond. I could be flippant with other people, I could lie to other people, but not her. Not while she sat on my desk, looking at me like, well, like she always looked at me. Like I was her person.

"I don't know," I said. And that was the truth. Even with all of the time spent trying to get even one of my questions answered, I was still coming up empty.

She smiled and took a sip of her coffee. I focused on the mug for a second; she used the same one every single day and the familiarity of it brought me some sort of comfort.

"I'm here," she said as she gave me one last smile before she walked back to her desk. There would be plenty of times in the future she would press the issue of making me talk, to the point of me getting angry (I'm pretty sure I threw my phone against a wall at one point), but this was not one of them. She knew I wasn't ready and that there was nothing to say. I know people wanted answers; believe me, I did too, but they weren't there. And wouldn't be.

Until Vanderbilt.

CHAPTER FIVE

The Doctor and the 'Lammies'
February 2015

It's hard to believe in luck while subsequently not believing in God. At least it is for me. This is why I am hard-pressed to use words like "karma" or "fate." Instead, I choose to subscribe to the idea that life is just a series of happenstances. Sure, I've blamed the universe for situations a time or two, but I don't really believe that has anything to do with it. Sometimes, it's just easier to shake my fist in the air like an old man yelling at the neighborhood kids to "get off his lawn," and curse the world for all the shit in my life.

Seriously, shake your fist in the air the next time you're pissed. It's great.

Keeping that in mind, when I was told one of only a handful of doctors in the country who knew what LAM was worked right here in Nashville, there was a moment where I thought maybe I was lucky. I mean, as lucky as a thirty-two-year-old who has a rare lung disease with no cure can be. The doctor who had so maliciously put in my chest tube called me one afternoon to let me know.

"I found you a LAM doctor," she said. I could hear the excitement in her voice. It calmed me. "And she's right here in

Nashville. At Vanderbilt."

I knew of Vanderbilt; most people in the medical profession do. A massive teaching hospital and one of the most prestigious facilities in the country. If anything, I'd had dreams of working at Vanderbilt one day; I had no desire to be a patient there.

"Thank you for everything." I hung up the phone and sank into the couch.

I knew this was a good thing.

I knew it was going to finally give me some fucking answers. Or rather, I assumed it would. I had this vision of going into the office and having the specialist spew out so much information I would be physically exhausted in the best way. Information overload from a real doctor and not some Internet doctor who went to the Upstairs Hollywood School of Medicines. Good, bad, ugly, or straight up shitty, I was going to have some clue about what was going on inside my body. And what that meant for the rest of my life.

Or even just for tomorrow.

The next four weeks would be an excruciating waiting game, but at least it felt like it was for a purpose.

* * * * * * *

Vanderbilt Hospital is massive. My only previous experience with the Vanderbilt campus was picking up a friend from her night shift one morning and even then, I remember feeling as if I was being swallowed by a sea of concrete. But it's not even the outside that is the most overwhelming. The size and vast expanse truly hits you the first time you walk through the doors.

Going into a teaching hospital is a different vibe. It is almost as if everyone knows you are there because there is something medically fucked up about you and, as a result, they treat you kinder than most. They smile, maintain eye contact, walk you where you need to go. Even if they are overworked and under-paid, they don't show it. Instead, they allow the people who walk through the doors the ability to exhale and be slightly less anxious about what will be discovered about their health.

The pulmonary office was in the basement and almost appeared as it had been forgotten from the rest of the hospital. The waiting room was decorated with '90s décor, something I found oddly comforting, likely because it reminded me of some of the best times of my life. In that moment, I was glad the look of clean lines and light greys had not made its way to this particular waiting room. I checked in and took a seat between Dan and the friend who had brought me to the hospital all those months ago.

Anyway, I sat in silence and tried to focus on whatever HGTV show was playing in the background. My companions didn't even attempt to talk to me, and I was happy for the moment of respite. I had nothing to say, and I don't think my brain was in a place where a coherent sentence could have been strung together. They both knew me well enough by now to know attempting to start some inane conversation would be an exercise in futility, so there we sat.

Eventually I was called back to have a round of testing done called a pulmonary function test. I won't bore you with all the details but picture a glass phone booth with a stool in it. You sit on the stool with a clip on your nose and blow into a mouthpiece.

Also, as a quick aside, I feel I should let you know—to save you from any embarrassment should you find yourself in a glass phone booth with a clip on your nose—that your respiratory therapist will *not* laugh if he says:

"Put your lips around it and blow."

And you respond with...

"That's what she said."

Instead, he will look at you like you just peed in his Cheerios and position his computer monitor so it is facing away from you for the remainder of the test.

I spent the next twenty-ish minutes taking short breaths, followed by long breaths, followed by holding my breath, followed by taking a three second breath, and then exhaling a four and a half second breath. Okay, maybe that is a tad exaggerated, but it's not too far off.

Once I felt like I had no air left in my lungs, I was moved to an exam room where Angie and Dan sat waiting and discussing their fear of a gigantic oxygen tank that sat in the corner. While my mind was clearly elsewhere, it did have quite an unnerving appearance; what I picture a small missile to look like. They looked at me and smiled, and I entered the room and took a seat next to the ominous tank.

"It wouldn't be good if that exploded," Dan said with a small smirk. His presence was physically comforting, but in this particular moment, his attempts at changing the subject left a little to be desired.

Angie snapped a photo next to the missile, for posterity of course, and then we all sat staring at each other with nothing left to say.

This was it. Good or bad, I was finally going to get some answers.

I tried to picture what my doctor was going to look like. Even with my newly developed hobby of spending hours trolling the Internet in search of "research," I had not looked her up. Let's be real, I'm dramatic as fuck and was really looking forward to the big reveal. I imagined her with a thick accent and a high and tight bun with streaks of grey. (I had been watching a lot of *Dawson's Creek* reruns at that time, so really, I was just picturing Jen Lindley's Grams.)

It was not Grams.

Instead, I was eventually greeted by a short, sweet, brunette woman with a gentle voice and kind eyes.

"I'm Dr. Young. It's nice to meet you."

Meeting her was going to change my life to the point that I

would sob after receiving her personal phone call a few years later to let me know she was leaving Vanderbilt.

But I'm getting ahead of myself.

I stuck out my hand and was met with a firm handshake and a smile. She was winning points already. Nothing was worse than a limp handshake. Well, maybe a rare and incurable lung disease would be worse, but a limp handshake is a close second. (An unexpected mushy grape is third.)

I know this next thing as both a patient and a nurse—and it isn't always true, but it's certainly not rare either.

Doctors talk *at* you, almost as if they are looking through you. Sometimes, I think it's because they are so smart, they lack the social skills it takes to converse with patients. Other times, I think it's because they truly can't be bothered. Either way, it happens regularly, and it's something you learn to expect when you are meeting with a doctor, especially a new one.

This was not the case with Dr. Young. It was the complete opposite and something I had only seen on TV dramas based in hospitals. Almost immediately, she took a seat next to me and began to talk like we were just two friends meeting over coffee. I never felt rushed or like I was asking a stupid question.

"It could be anything. Emphysema, asthma, another less rare lung disease."

"Really?" I felt my heartbeat quicken and knew the excitement of this being anything other than what I thought it was had caused my voice to increase by several decibels.

"Yes, it could be. But..."

Fuck.

"But, I have a feeling it's LAM."

The hope left the room as quickly as it arrived.

"Unfortunately, I can't give an answer today."

My heart sank. Right into my asshole. You've got to be kidding me. That was the entire point of today. Answers. Instead, I had no hope and no answers. Fantastic.

I did my best to hold back the tears that wanted so badly to flow as she continued. "There is a little more to getting you a definitive diagnosis than your CT scan and lung function results. It's a blood test."

Okay. One more vial of blood was needed. One more tiny bit of blood was all that was left. How long could that take? One day, maybe two if they didn't put a rush on it. I could handle that.

Too bad that wasn't exactly how this was going to go down.

Turns out, the blood work required to diagnose had to be sent to a lab that apparently didn't understand that my very sanity depended on the results, so I was looking at another two- to three-week waiting period, at the very least.

"That's okay. It's already been a couple of months. What's a few more weeks?" Did my voice just break at the end of that sentence?

It sure did. Shit. My acting skills were not up to par that particular day and instead of a smile and a sarcastic comment, my defeat decided to present itself all over my now tear-stained face.

She put her hand on my shoulder. "I know this is hard. But this is the next step. And hopefully the last."

We talked about a few more things that were likely, the possibility of a biopsy if the blood work was inconclusive (fuck all that), and then I was off to get blood drawn and wait some more.

Oh, goody.

If I wasn't a woman on the brink of a complete meltdown, I certainly would have been during the next few weeks while I waited for the fate of my future to be determined by a little vial of blood. Had I been at all lucky, someone who loved me would have had me committed and I could have enjoyed the next few weeks highly medicated and blissfully unaware. Sadly, the medical community looks down on having individuals with no acute mental health issues medicated to the point of oblivion, so I had to wait it out on my own.

Instead, I had to suck it up and get through it on my own. Like a fucking peasant. I spent the next month on complete autopilot.

Go to work. Drink beer. Shoot liquor. Go to sleep. Repeat.

Once again, I had been thrust into health purgatory and my only option was to wait. Oh, and lubricate my brain with tequila and Miller Lite.

And then it happened. Somewhere between beers and breakdowns, I finally got my answer. One evening, a phone call came through from Dr. Young, something I knew to be a bad sign. Doctors don't call themselves if the answers are benign, only if the results aren't good. I always thought it was funny that people got mad when the doctor didn't call with their results personally.

Trust me, you want the nurse on the other end of that line.

I didn't get the nurse.

Despite her calming voice, I found myself wishing it was anyone else's voice that I heard that night.

I feigned some small talk, asked how she was doing. Not because I was being disingenuous, but because I wanted to relish the last few moments of my life before LAM likely became an official part of my makeup.

A definitive diagnosis meant I would know the answer to the three-month-old question that had kept me up most every night.

But it would also mean my life would be changed forever, and not in a good way.

She told me I had LAM that evening.

I hung up the phone but I didn't cry. I thought I was going to feel an overwhelming sense of sadness once I knew and that the tears that had come so easily before would be tenfold. Instead, I felt relief. Not because my life was not going to be difficult, but because the giant question mark that had taken up residence in my brain had finally become a period.

* * * * * * *

Amidst all of the chaos of what was now a definite diagnosis, and more nervous breakdowns that I could count, there were some glimmers of hope that began to peek through what had been a bleak couple of months. One of those moments came from (I can't believe I am saying this) a Facebook group.

Most days I hate Facebook. It has quickly become an arena for everyone to air their political views, religious beliefs, multi-level-marketing schemes, and overall douche-baggery. Gone are the simpler times of the "dot edu" email requirement, which brought with it pictures of keg stands, and statuses bitching about the ten-page paper due the following day that you had not even begun.

Now, Facebook is flooded with individuals who are more than happy to post their ill-informed opinions on social media, and then condemn anyone who disagrees with them.

And the originality of a status update? A thing of the past sans a few witty friends who don't post nearly often enough to drown out the noise with their quips and humor. Instead, I am left to mindlessly scroll through posts such as:

Fuck [insert president], status

#Blessed, status

Super vague fishing for sympathy, status

Picture of food/pet/booze, status (this one, I am 100% guilty of)

Needless to say, I can count on one hand the reasons I keep Facebook in my life.

Lammies is one of those reasons.

I had been left pretty discouraged after my first Vanderbilt appointment. I was not used to doctors having minimal answers, especially doctors at one of the best medical facilities in the country. They were scientists, and teachers, and cared about helping people, all of which requires a pretty solid percentage of certainty.

In the case of my diagnosing physician, and I assume all doctors who work in the rare disease field, it was not due to a lack of knowledge. It was due to a lack of patients. Just to throw some numbers at you, roughly three in one million women (and one man) have a confirmed LAM diagnosis. Not only does it make the disease extremely rare, but it also makes trending any sort of similarities difficult because each case is "just different enough." What does that do for a physician? It forces them to answer "I don't know" to too many of your questions, which I can't imagine feels good for them either.

For me it felt like a kick in the crotch.

While she couldn't provide me solace (which I understand is totally not her job, but still...), she informed me that there was a group on Facebook that I may find helpful. She scribbled the word "Lammies" on a Post-it note and told me that she thought this may help.

I had never been more excited to have a piece of paper in my hand. Maybe excited is not the right word. Relieved would be more accurate. I had spent the last few months talking about my disease to people who could only empathize. Finally, I was going to be around women who got me. Who I could ask questions. Who could sympathize. Who were as jaded and angry as I was.

Well. The first three were spot on. The anger? Turns out, I would have to look elsewhere.

Somehow, all of the women on the page seemed to have come to terms with their diagnosis. They called each other "sisters." They were kind. They were optimistic. They were accepting. All of the things I wasn't, and to be honest, am still not. And I didn't understand. I was caught in the purgatory between anger and depression and here were these women, lifting each other up and sharing their stories when all I wanted to do was say,

I'm fucking pissed, how about you?

But I didn't. Instead, I read each welcome message from Lammies around the world, wondering if I would ever reach a place where I considered my diagnosis a sisterhood and not just a curse.

Disclaimer: I haven't. I'm still angry as hell. And I still feel alone.

The solitary extrovert. How poetic.

In addition to the lack of anger present, there is another caveat to the Lammies page; one that I hadn't considered until the day it happened. I am not sure why it didn't cross my mind, but it didn't, which allowed me to be completely blindsided when it happened. While I didn't have it in me to post any words of encouragement, I had come to value the knowledge of the ladies on the page. No one ever uttered the words "I don't know." If they didn't have an answer, they let you know of someone who did.

And then, just when I let my guard down, it happened.

Someone died.

I'll never forget it. Mostly because she was twenty-seven.

Twenty. Fucking. Seven.

And the thing that killed her had taken up residence in my lungs like an apartment squatter.

Remember that time people liked to offer solutions to my "can't have a baby problem?" Well, turns out, they also like to put their two cents in when you are hyperventilating at work because you are convinced you are going to be the next to die à la Final Destination.

Well, you don't know what else was wrong with her.

Your case is different.

You've got a long life ahead of you.

And my absolute favorite?

They will find a cure before you die.

These are the legitimate nuggets of "comfort" I was offered

as I was embarrassingly weeping at my desk, questioning how long I had to live. To be clear, I'm not mocking people's attempts at comfort, although I can see how it seems that way. It's just one of those things: the struggle between knowing people are trying to be kind and wanting to shake someone and say, "You don't think I've heard all of this before?"

Not to mention, I was not a huge fan of empty promises. Never had been. I much prefer silence.

Eventually, I found my way outside, standing under a tree, smoking one of the many cigarettes I would smoke before I finally quit for good (sorry, Mom, I kind of lied about that). I wanted to go home and curl up into a little ball and spend the rest of the day wallowing in my own self-pity. I didn't. Mostly because my PTO had been tied up in my procedure to have my tubes tied up. (Cheap joke, I know.)

But I spent the rest of the day thinking about death and wondering if mine was looming on the horizon.

Speculating about what "forever" feels like after you're gone and how I wasn't even close to being ready for my life to be over. I thought about my mother and how she would handle life if she had to bury her child. And I was scared as hell; petrified that I had left no mark on the world and I would die in mediocrity.

Now, some years later, I can say that I have found some semblance of community by being a part of the Lammies page. I have realized that you can have a sense of community and still feel alone. I like to believe I am not the only one on the page who feels the same way. But I am thankful for these women. Mostly because they have the strength to do what I am still not ready to do .

To ask the hard questions.

To put themselves and their stories out there amongst the only people on the planet who "get it."

To challenge themselves to do things they may have never done before, because we (the LAM patients) really don't know what is in store for us down the road.

I hold Lammies very close to me. And despite my being silent on the page, the page is *not* silent in my life. And the deaths still hit me, some harder than others. But I no longer shy away from the page, despite some recommendations that I should because it "just depresses you." That is only partially true. There is sadness on the page, of course. That comes with the territory.

But, the sadness keeps me grounded in reality. Reminds me that a fear of death doesn't make it inevitable.

CHAPTER SIX

The Sex Part

Sex.

Giggles to herself

I needed to say the word once and get it out of the way. So that I can transition into this next part a little easier. Mature, I know, but as progressive as I am in my views, that doesn't mean I don't feel like a sixth-grader in health class when I am trying to talk about it on a larger scale and to an audience that is exponentially bigger than my group of girlfriends.

Even though I *know* how important it is to talk about it, I really, really, really want to pretend that this next part isn't my reality. That sex could just be something I got to keep between the person I was sleeping with and myself.

Sometimes, just myself, if I'm feeling particularly ambitious.

But I am going to talk about it. In a second. So, enjoy some exposition while I work up the nerve.

For most of my adult life, I have tried to be at least a realist, if not the occasional optimist. Pessimism made me sleepy, realism made me feel content, and optimism was a nice little vacation from reality. While realism was where I spent the majority of time, there were certainly days when I was so happy I wanted to sing show tunes in the middle of the street. Sober. I mean, anyone can sing show tunes in public after enough lemon drop shots, but when I was feeling optimistic, I would have done it after one cup of coffee and a smile from a stranger.

In my twenties, I was perpetually single with an amazing group of girlfriends and a male entourage who would kill anyone who hurt me. Literally. They have threatened several of the less than stellar men I allowed into my life. On top of that, I had a family who was always supportive of me, regardless of my intermittent piss-poor life choices, and I even managed to take an entry-level receptionist position at a medical company and parlay it into a nursing career.

I was far from having my shit together, but overall things were good.

Seriously, stick with me, the sex part is coming. I'm just stalling. Because I can feel the vomit forming just thinking about writing this down. But I promise I'm getting there. Just give me a minute.

Anyway.

There was nothing I could have imagined would have been catastrophic enough to cause the shift from occasional optimist to pessimist. Although, I suppose most people who aren't constantly depressed could not fathom a situation that would cause them to be miserable almost daily after spending so much time carefree and giving close to zero fucks.

I didn't realize it had happened at first. I knew I was a different person, but I didn't think I had acquired a different view of life overall. It wasn't until a discussion (or, more accurately, a fight) with Dan shortly after my definitive diagnosis that I first realized that more than my health had been, and was going to be, affected by the recent and swift decline in my lung function.

The fight went something like this:

Me: Sarcastic comment.

Dan: Defensive comment.

Me: Sarcastic comment but louder.

Dan: Silence.

Me: Yelling even louder about who knows what.

And then Dan did something he had never done before and has done very rarely since. He said exactly what he was thinking.

"You're not the same person you were before," he said. The words were cutting.

"Excuse me?"

I had phrased it as a question, but it was not because I wanted a response. The words hurt almost as much as my first chest tube and I wanted an explanation for his sudden desire to be honest instead of suppress his feelings.

Eight words.

Eight little words that, at first, made me so angry I couldn't see straight. I mean, how dare he? Of course, I'm not the same person. How could I be? And even if he thought that, what a set of brass balls he had to say it out loud. To my face.

Great, I thought. Of all the issues our relationship faced, now I had to worry about putting on a happy face.

Anyone who knows me knows that I don't bullshit. That is, of course, with the exception of the six- to twelve-month honeymoon period in a new relationship when I pretend that I don't poop, fart, throw up because I drank too much, and where I act like nothing makes me angry and that I wake up looking airbrushed and with fresh breath.

That six-month relationship me and everyday me does not hold herself to the same standard in my everyday relationships; I am unapologetically honest, even when it would better serve me, and everyone else involved, to shut up and keep things to myself. If I wasn't the person I was when we started dating, I was going to have to attempt to act like the person I used to be, which would prove especially difficult since I didn't even realize I had changed that drastically.

The mere thought was exhausting. But, after I got over the initial anger at what Dan had said, I realized that he had a point. I absolutely wasn't the same person. And didn't he deserve the person he fell in love with? For everything he'd put up with, the least I could do was try to act like my personality shift was just a temporary short circuit and I had the ability to evolve back into the girl I was. And hey, maybe if I faked it long enough, it would eventually turn into the truth.

Hell. If I could switch the way I put the toilet paper on the holder for him, I could certainly train myself to revert back to my old personality. Seems rational and totally doable.

So, that's exactly what I did. Was it a flawless transition? Not exactly. But I really was trying. I spent each and every minute mindful of every word I said, every facial expression, every action and reaction. I made every effort to act like I wasn't angry. Or severely depressed. Or extremely lost. I would wait until he was gone and I then I would try to get every pent-up feeling out of my system before he got back.

Around people, I was together. Calm. Back to "normal." When I was alone, I screamed, cried, punched things. Threw the occasional plate.

I tried to go back to enjoying the "little things" even though I felt like I should be doing something greater. To act like a sunny day made me smile, or an accolade at work was enough to make my day.

It was exhausting.

What is worse than being a pessimist? Being a pessimist trying to be an optimist. I was not only angry, but I was beginning to resent both myself and the people around me who made me feel like I had to act this way.

It was at this point that I decided that therapy may be a good investment (duh). For the sake of wanting to feel like a better person, let's pretend I came to that conclusion all on my own and not because I failed at the big fake and was basically told something had to give. I was not opposed to therapy; I had been going on and off my entire life. But this situation was different. I wouldn't even know where to begin. And I wasn't entirely sure I had the capability to let therapy have the positive effect it had inspired in the past.

But I went. Not for me (at first). But as a favor to the people in my life who longed for me to move past all of my anger and resentment. Little did I know it was going to throw me headfirst into a giant pool of repressed feelings and sexual confusion.

It would seem that among all of the problems I was acquiring like Garbage Pail Kids cards, sex was one of them.

It warrants saying one more time that I cannot stress enough how little I wanted to put these thoughts down on paper. I'm not a prude by any means (for all the people who knew me in my twenties, keep the details to yourself), but putting my sex life out there for everyone to judge is a difficult thing to do. As much as I would like to gloss over this very real issue, I would be doing a disservice to myself and to everyone reading this if I was not completely transparent.

Buckle up. We're going to talk about sex. And not in a fun way.

*Okay, Mom. Please stop reading. I promise you aren't going to miss anything if you head right on over to the next chapter. For the sake of our relationship, and mostly my dignity, please stop.

Okay. If you're still reading, it's on you now. Just don't tell me.

Anyway...

The sexual issues that occurred due to LAM were two-fold. The first began the day my lung collapsed. Dan and I had had sex the night before. It was not illogical that, as a result, there was a fear that the increased activity had assisted or caused my pneumothorax. Now, before you start to say things like, "But you're a nurse," or "You know better," let me be clear. A pneumothorax followed by a diagnosis that, for all intents and purposes, will eventually kill you, is a traumatic event. So, logic, much like hindsight, is 20/20. Years later, I understand that having sex did not cause my lung to collapse but, at the time, you could not have convinced myself or Dan otherwise.

Not having sex (if you were having sex before) takes a toll on a relationship. Sex can be amazing with someone you don't ever plan on seeing again. Yes, I said it. And it's true. But, when I am in a relationship, sex adds trust, romance, and passion to a relationship. It also makes fighting not so bad. When that is suddenly removed, it can have a detrimental effect on the couple. My fear dissipated much quicker than Dan's did. Make no mistake, I don't fault him for this and, especially as I am writing, I can absolutely understand his trepidation. At the time, I was not nearly as empathetic.

Once I realized that sex could be back on the table, I wanted it. Not in a pervy way, but in a "we are working through a hard time together and intimacy would make me feel good" kind of way. And maybe in a little bit of a pervy way; for fun.

Unfortunately, Dan was not in the same headspace. I don't know why I expected him to be or why I felt as if he should be on my timeline and my timeline alone, but I was not thrilled at my newfound celibacy. I felt like I had a roommate, not a partner. I wondered if I was no longer attractive, if he wanted out of the relationship. Mostly, I wondered if we would ever get to a place where we would have sex ever again.

I hate that I was so angry at him for feeling like he did. And it's not like he wasn't honest about it. I just didn't believe him. I already felt as if I was damaged. Like being a kid and wanting a pair of Air Jordans and your parents got you the Kmart version instead. Why would he want to have sex with me? I was broken.

Down the rabbit hole I went, getting to a place of such self-loathing that I legitimately thought of leaving him. For his own good. And for mine a bit, as well.

I could just move to a town where no one knew me and

have sex without feelings and without concern.

Yup. That's exactly how sex works. Especially for women.

And how love works.

And how life works.

Clearly, I didn't leave. I didn't actually want to. Dan without sex is better than life without Dan. But my brain did not compute that at the time. What we should have done was go to a therapist and work through each of our fears and issues. Unfortunately, it would be another four years before I found my way to therapy. At some point, we got back into our routine, so to speak. Somewhere along the way, we were able to make our way to back to each other. Unfortunately, this shift towards normalcy would be brief.

For a majority of the time after diagnosis and after several more health scares (don't worry, that hot mess is coming up), sex was the furthest thing from my mind. There were days that I couldn't walk from the couch to the bathroom without wanting to pass out, so clearly any additional strenuous activity was off the table initially. I expected I would have to work towards getting my lung function back to where it was, but I did not for a moment believe that my significant decrease in lung function was permanent.

When it became clear that my lung function had plateaued, I had to admit to myself that I didn't have to acknowledge it if I just didn't exercise. And really, sex is exercise, if you're doing it right. I was going to have to talk about sex on oxygen.

And I wanted to die.

I certainly wasn't going to ask this question on the Facebook page. I would sooner shit in my hands and clap.

And I couldn't ask Dan. He would say he didn't care if I had to be on oxygen. While I believe him, there is nothing inherently sexy about the continuous hum of an oxygen concentrator and the idea of tubing getting tangled God-knows-where. Not an option.

But not having sex was also not an option.

So.

I decided to ask my doctor.

And let me tell you what. There is nothing more humbling than receiving treatment at one of the best hospitals in the country, by one of the smartest minds in the pulmonary fields, and having to ask her if "doggy style" would be a better position for my breathing.

It is, by the way. If I have to know that, so do you.

But I did ask. And she was great. Told me I wasn't the only one who had these concerns. If she was lying, I couldn't tell. God, I hoped she wasn't lying. And she then offered me some alternatives.

Have you ever wondered what it's like to feel like a real prostitute?

Simple. Get told that you can have sex but without kissing on the mouth.

Wouldn't be as hard of a pill to swallow if I could attach that act with a dollar amount. (Yeah, I said it.) But I'm not a prostitute. I'm a woman who just wants to have an intimate moment or two with her boyfriend without him feeling like he's fucking an invalid.

We do have sex. Not often, but enough. That's mostly on me. It's because I had a hard enough time being comfortable naked without adding oxygen tubing into the mix. But you can't be great in bed while you can't breathe. Trust me. I've tried.

"You okay?" Dan will always ask.

"Of course," I will respond, whether I am okay or not.

Instead, I just had to lie there and know that if I could just get over myself, my sex life would be a little more interesting. Sometimes, after I do all of my lying there, I cry in the bathroom afterwards like I did when the guy I lost my virginity to screwed me over.

I still haven't said anything on the Facebook page. Can't bring myself to admit that I think sex is as important as it is. Even though it is.

But more than that, if I can feel normal in one aspect of my life, I want it to be during sex with my partner. My person. If I put my pride aside and donned my oxygen, I could have sex like a wife and not like a hooker. (Okay, maybe just a little bit like a hooker.) But then that would mean LAM has crept into my bedroom and taken up permanent residence there. I'm clearly not ready for that.

I will likely come to a place where I will have to choose between sex with oxygen and no sex at all. And when I get there, I'll figure it out. But until then, I just can't allow my diagnosis to take "normal" sex away from me. Dammit. From *us*.

LAM doesn't get to join our sex life; I may not be a prude, but I'm definitely not into threesomes.

Unless it's his birthday.

(Kidding. That's what you get for reading this entire chapter, Mom. Because I know you did.)

CHAPTER SEVEN

The National Institutes of Health
October, 2015

I couldn't for the life of me figure out why I'd agreed to this. I'm sure there was someone I could have blamed other than myself, had I been in my normal state of mind.

But I wasn't. Far from it.

I was sitting alone at an airport just outside of Washington, D.C., waiting for a shuttle that was going to take me to a place I didn't even want to go. I debated walking back inside and catching the next flight back to Nashville. As I weighed the pros and cons, the bus marked "NIH" pulled up to the curb. There was no turning back now. I took a seat near the front of the bus, across from a couple who I could tell immediately had done this before. The wife looked at me and smiled, the husband just sat staring forward. He was clearly the patient.

I'd wished I'd brought someone with me. My pride had not allowed that, however, and I agreed to go, but only if I could do it on my own.

"It's no big deal," I'd lied to each person who had offered their company. And there had been several.

Turns out, it was. I felt completely isolated and the company, any company, would have kept my brain at least somewhat preoccupied. But it was clearly too late for that. I picked up my phone to call Dan for at least some solace, but quickly decided against it. No one wants to be *that* person on a bus.

Instead, I made polite small talk with a woman across the aisle who it turned out was the wife of a patient. Normally, I would have put my headphones on and pretended to sleep, but we were on a bus that was headed to the same unknown outcome and we both needed a kind ear. Turns out, her husband had been diagnosed with an extremely rare brain tumor and they had been going to NIH for several years. The tumor had caused a significant change to his personality, and not for the better. You could tell by looking into his eyes that something was off.

It was almost unnerving. Yet, there she sat. By his side. Clearly exhausted but also still in love with the man she married, despite the fact that his illness had caused him not to be that man anymore. She asked about my diagnosis, and not in the annoying way that most people do because they are nosy, but out of genuine concern. I told her the name and like everyone before her, she told me that she'd never heard of it.

"It's okay. No one ever has." That phrase had quickly become my go-to response to anyone who told me that my diagnosis was something unknown to them. As I usually did, I added a smile at the end of the sentence so I seemed genuine. I certainly did not want to appear bitchy. Not that I didn't mean what I was saying, it had just become second nature to me, like breathing. Or sarcasm.

We chatted for a couple more minutes before her husband required her attention. I turned to face the window just as the infamous NIH came into view. As the campus grew closer and closer, I couldn't help but be almost speechless at the landscape that had seemed to appear out of nowhere and into view.

The vastness of the NIH campus is indescribable, but I will do my best to make my fifth grade teacher proud of my impeccable descriptive skills. Vanderbilt paled in comparison to the hospital that seemed to stretch for miles. In my head I pictured a sprawling grey landscape with concrete buildings menacingly looking down at all of the new patients. Instead, the grounds were warm and inviting with green hills and pink flowers surrounding each building. While the size was intimidating, the scenery was inviting and managed to decrease a tad of my anxiety.

The main building sat like a beacon in the center of the campus, and I learned that would be my home for the next three days. The bus stopped in front of the building and before I got off, I turned to say goodbye to my new friend. I hadn't realized it, but her small talk had helped calm me down, even if only a little bit. She smiled and wished me luck as the doors closed.

I wonder about her still, and her husband.

Did they get the answers they were looking for? I hope so.

I followed the sidewalk to the main entrance and I walked through the front doors, awkwardly wheeling my suitcase behind me. When I entered the building, I stood for a moment, taking it all in. Few things live up to the grandeur of their names, but the NIH was an exception. The "lobby" was the size of a large mall and almost had the same aesthetic. White coats peppered the hallways and the men and women who donned the coats looked particularly "scientific" as they walked from one place to the other.

I was very obviously in the presence of some of the smartest people in the world, so much so that you could feel it.

I wandered around the expansive interior before I eventually found my way to the check-in area. I was briefly mistaken for an eighteen-year-old deaf patient (I thought sign language was just a service they offered but appreciated the mistake in my age), I was found by the correct staff member who had been tasked with taking me to my unit. The elevator ride was quiet, but I had no doubt my guide had done this countless times and could read the room well enough to know I was too overwhelmed to speak. Instead, we stood together in silence and I counted the "bings" that marked each floor we passed. The doors finally opened and with a smile, she led me onto the unit.

The eighth floor looked like any other hospital floor, which was actually a welcome surprise. It allowed me to forget the massive nature of the hospital. I could pretend that I was some-where else, a normal people hospital, instead of feeling swal-lowed up by the magnitude of my situation. After a quick tour of the floor, I was taken to my room. Oddly enough, despite how alone I felt, I was somewhat put out by the fact that I had a roommate. I had participated in enough small talk on the shuttle; I wanted to be left alone at night to wallow in my own self-pity.

My roommate introduced herself in a thick Minnesota ac-cent that put a smile on my face. We exchanged pleasantries and disease names and then she was off for testing, something that would quickly become familiar to me. I settled into my bed, thankful it was furthest from the door, and closed my eyes to rest. Almost instantly, the first member of the nonstop testing parade came into my room. I was given my twenty-four-hour urine collection container, the test that would prove to be the most annoying, and my schedule for my three-day stay.

I perused the list of tests as I answered standard questions and had my vital signs taken. MRIs; complete bone scans; CTs; pulmonary function tests; exercise testing; the list went on. I realized quickly that rest would not be easily obtainable and the thought instantly made me sleepy. The nurse finished my initial assessment and was off to do more important things, but not before letting me know there were several other LAM patients on the floor if I wanted to meet them before our meet-ing that evening.

I smiled politely while silently declining. If I had learned one thing from the LAM support group Facebook page, it was that most of the women with the diagnosis were oddly optimistic. I'd be lying if I didn't say I found it slightly annoying at times, especially when LAM was referred to as a sisterhood, but it was a level of acceptance I envied. Perhaps it's because for me, the diagnosis was still so new, but I certainly didn't feel privileged to be a LAM patient and I didn't feel like faking that feeling.

A few more staff members trickled in and out and before I knew it, it was time for our "round table" discussion. To my recollection, only one woman there was younger than me; the rest were in their fifties. I learned quickly that as far as the diagnosis spectrum, I was one of the younger patients to be diagnosed.

Lucky me.

The remainder of the meeting was mostly centered on the logistics of our stay and how the data would be used to "help cure LAM." We were excused from the meeting and while several patients and their family members hung back, I couldn't wait to get back to my room and get some sleep. Luckily, my roommate was already asleep and I noticed she'd left a cupcake on my windowsill. I changed into my pajamas, took a few bites, and drifted off to sleep. I knew tomorrow would do one of two things: (1.) give me too much information or (2.) give me hope. I was keeping my fingers crossed for the latter.

* * * * * * *

If I was a paranoid schizophrenic, I would have been convinced my body was being involuntarily donated to science or observed by extraterrestrials for posterity. I was awoken out of a dead sleep by a lab tech who had a second job as a vampire and felt compelled to drain me of all my blood. After taking twenty-one vials (this, for once, is not an exaggeration), she left and told me she'd be back tomorrow.

For what? I thought to myself. Normally, I would have said that out loud, but my sarcasm was clearly still asleep, as I should have been. I figured I may as well start my day. I peed in my giant jug, brushed my teeth, and tried not to wake my sleeping room companion. Breakfast came and went and soon it was time for the first stop in my myriad of testing. First came the chest x-ray followed by the bone scan,

(run back to my room to pee so I don't have to carry around a container of my urine everywhere I go) ...

...Followed by a CT, which was followed by a second CT, and for some reason, that one only worked if I drank a vat of Satan's semen (or contrast, if you'd rather) first.

At some point, not even sure what time of day it was by then, I made it back to my room and did my best to relax. I felt like a lab rat; like I should have been given a number so they could have tested me with complete anonymity. I may as well have been given a tank of oxygen and told to run through a maze.

At some point during the day, while I was being distracted with needles and scans, my roommate had apparently reached her threshold of testing and checked out. As sweet as she was, I was happy to have some solace and hoped that I would remain without a roommate for the last couple of days. My eyelids were heavy and I was happy to finally drift off to sleep. It was only forty-five minutes before my next test and while I had never been one who could take a power nap, it came quite easily in that moment.

Eventually, the day had come to an end. My mother had made the drive from New York to D.C. to see my uncles and provide moral support in the form of carbohydrates and company. Dan would be joining us the next day, along with my sister and her now husband. This would be the second time my health resulted in all of us being together; not the worst thing, but it would have been nice if my lungs were still normal.

Just saying.

Even the thought of dinner was stressful; I either had to

take my urine jug with me to the restaurant (nope), or hope that I didn't have to pee while I was off campus. I should have been relishing in the idea of stuffing myself full of authentic food and dry red wine, but instead, I couldn't stop thinking about my urine.

Enjoy your escargot and concentrated pee.

I did my best to act normal through dinner. I engaged in small talk and my family did their best to talk about anything else, which I must say, they had become almost flawless at since my diagnosis. I stuffed myself full of bread, cheese, and steak, and tried to imagine that I was going back to my uncle's home in the heart of D.C. instead of a sterile room in a giant hospital. Towards the end of the night, someone broke the ice.

"So, how is it?"

"It's interesting," I said, then paused, deciding if I wanted to say the next part. "But it's a lot."

My uncle took a sip of his wine and I longed for a taste, cursing myself for being responsible and ordering water with lemon, something I don't think I had ever done before in my life.

He held his cup up in the air and said, "Here's to getting some answers."

I tapped my water glass to his and said "Here's hoping" or something equally as passive-aggressive and vague as shit.

I'm not sure if it was the toast, or if I had suddenly realized I had to pee, but I felt myself quickly becoming overwhelmed. I wanted to crawl into bed and sleep as best I could until the next round of "activities." My kind Minnesotan roommate had been discharged and so I was more than happy to be returned to my room, piss in my bucket, and drift in and out of sleep while Keith Morrison's oddly soothing voice mentally rocked me back and forth.

It was probably a bad decision to leave the campus even though I thought it would make the experience easier. Seeing my family made me want to say "fuck it" and just leave and never look back. However, I couldn't help but think of all the women before me who were the reason I didn't have to shoot myself full of Progesterone. The women who gave me a twenty- to thirty-year life expectancy instead of a ten-year one. I would stay for those women, despite my desire to be completely self- ish.

* * * * * * *

I am convinced that any office that relates to pulmonology is purposely located at the end of an extremely long hallway. In fact, other than the office at Vanderbilt (which has since moved, to the end of a gigantic building), I have never been to a pul- monary office that was not up a set of stairs, down a long hall, and that leaves you breathless by the time you reach your destination. I've never asked, but I'm pretty sure this is on purpose.

NIH was no different.

We're so sorry your lungs are shitty. Really, we are. But why don't you walk half a mile down this ominous hallway?

Then put on a mask.

Then ride an exercise bike as long as you can.

While I ask you if "that's the best you can do."

As I walked the green mile, I pictured a bunch of doctors wearing the white coats I saw each doctor adorn on my first day. They would all be sitting in a room with one of those reverse mirrors from any detective show on television, and they would be watching all of the pulmonary patients on a secret camera; making bets about whether or not we made it all the way down the hallway; how many times we had to stop; snickering to themselves because they knew they could have had the office at the start of the hallway.

I can't prove this happened, but I can't say with 100% cer- tainty it didn't.

I was "greeted" by a doctor whose bedside manner left a

little to be desired. Luckily, I had been warned about his curt attitude before my visit, so I hadn't expected warm and fuzzy upon meeting him. He introduced himself, shook my hand, and explained the premise of the exercise test I would be performing.

My lack of ability to ride this bike has nothing to do with my piss-poor lungs, I thought. *It's the years of eating poorly, drinking excessively, and pretending that gyms didn't exist.*

He quickly left the room and I was glad he wouldn't be there to judge my laughable bike-riding.

As a whole, respiratory therapists have a great sense of humor. (I'd had one experience to the contrary, involving the therapist I mentioned before and his lack of appreciation for a good 'that's what she said' joke.) Usually, I found them easy to talk to, down to earth, and mildly sarcastic. It was a perfect combination of traits that made me dread pulmonary testing a little less.

The therapist smiled and handed me a mask to wear that made me look like the milk chocolate version of Hannibal Lecter. I thought about making the joke but it appeared that, while his eyes were kind, he was another therapist who would not have appreciated my dark humor.

As I looked at the contraption and tried to focus on my breathing, I wondered if anyone "passed" this particular test. Between the heart monitor, the scuba mask, and my lungs, I couldn't imagine there was any way I was going to make it more than five minutes.

FYI, I made it to six.

Suck it, Lance Armstrong.

My chipper physician was less than impressed. I believe the words "You failed because you are out of shape" were said, but I can't be positive.

* * * * * * *

65

I sat at a table with my treatment team to go over the results of all the testing. In the first five minutes, I'd learned I didn't have HIV, Hepatitis, STDs (all things I had been pretty positive of prior), and a myriad of other random ailments. But, I knew what was happening. They were giving me the good news before they hit me with the bad. It was a trick used in the medical field, and many others I'm sure, that I had used myself dozens of times.

I was right.

"The CT showed hundreds of cysts on your lungs. They are small, which is good, but too numerous to count."

The idea of tiny little invaders multiplying inside my body and covering the organ that helped me breathe gave me goosebumps. It's not like I hadn't known they were there—my doctor and Vanderbilt and my extensive Internet work had confirmed this—but I had not had a solid number before. If they were already too numerous to count, what were my lungs going to look like in five years? In ten?

I know that they continued to talk about prognosis, possible medical interventions, and possible clinical trials, but, other that knowing the true progression of my disease, my mind was only on one thing. I waited for a break in the conversation and then blurted out my question.

"So, kids? Yes or no?" There was no time for witty banter or a well-placed segue.

The treatment team glanced at each other across the table.

"In your case?" The doctor who had seemed so cold during my bicycle excursion suddenly had a look of pity in his eyes and had seemingly transformed into a caring and empathetic provider. I knew immediately what his answer was going to be at that moment and yet, I was still extremely ill-prepared.

"No." Clearly, he was taking my cue and not offering any sort of segue.

"Given the progression of your disease, I don't see pregnancy being something you should risk."

The team said nothing, but their looks told me they agreed. Well, there it was.

I shouldn't have been alone for this part. Someone should have been with me to hold my hand. Literally. Once again, I had to remind myself that my pride was to blame for my non-existent companionship in this particular moment, and not for a lack of trying by the people in my life. I smiled but said nothing. I was afraid if I opened my mouth to speak, the tears would come just like they had so many times before in the past year.

There was no way I was going to ugly cry at the NIH.

While making the effort to maintain my composure and appear nonchalant, I had a realization. An epiphany, if I want to be douchey about it. Did I want answers? Sure. But that's not the entire reason I was at the NIH.

And it wasn't for the women before me.

Or the women after. It wasn't for posterity.

It wasn't for the clinical trials.

It wasn't even for an accurate timeline of my life expectancy.

It was simply so I could be (painfully) aware of all the things I was going to lose.

CHAPTER EIGHT

The Babies

Much like an orgasm on a first date (or for the entire duration of several relationships), I faked this chapter the first time. I had it written in its entirety before the version you are about to read. It was my typical mix of sarcasm and judgement...

(some professionals might refer to those traits as my defense mechanisms, but I drown them out with whiskey)

...and it only lightly skimmed the surface of what it is like to have an outside influence force you to make a life-altering decision. After some time passed, I came back and I read over what I had written. I was not impressed. It felt superficial and hollow, and was not the level of honesty that I vowed would be the focus of this book.

Initially, I put down the words I thought would make me look like a better, more put-together person instead of writing down everything that I never said out loud because I thought it made me look like a shit. Hiding my true feelings about not being a mother doesn't do anything but make it seem like my feelings were wrong. And they weren't. And still aren't.

So, that chapter is gone; deleted. I couldn't even begin to

tell you what was contained within it, because it was all bull-shit. Not one genuine sentence.

I can't care about being scared or vulnerable, just because this is likely the rawest I will have to be.

Instead, I am going to put my thoughts down on paper as if I am the only one who will ever read the words. That is the only way what you read will be real and honest. Because it will not be white-washed or peppered with poorly timed puns and well-placed swear words.

(Well, maybe one or two swear words, just so you don't forget how much I love them.)

These are the thoughts of a woman who was told she cannot perform the bodily function that has been engrained in us since childhood. The thing we are literally made for. This is every thought that came into my head the day I sat in that room at NIH and was told I could never have children.

With a LAM diagnosis, or I assume after any new and potentially deadly diagnosis, there is a period of all things unknown, followed by (at least) some answers. But only some. Even with a label, when a rare disease is discovered, uncertainty still reigns supreme. One of the few contributors to LAM pathology that the medical community seems to agree on is that estrogen is the driving force behind the advancement of the disease. So, in addition to the mere fact that I am female, other factors that can increase estrogen include birth control, certain foods (I am totally okay with the fact that I can't eat tofu), and pregnancy.

A large number of women are diagnosed after they have already given birth; oftentimes because they suffer a lung collapse during pregnancy or shortly after. To me, these women are lucky. Of course, some may believe I am playing it a bit fast and loose with the word "lucky." But, I think about how grateful I would have been to have at least one child before I knew that pregnancy could advance my disease to the point of no return. I do not usually believe that naivete gets you anywhere, but in this case, it could have potentially gotten me to motherhood.

That would have been nice.

Really fucking nice.

But clearly, that's not what happened.

Now, if we were looking at my history surrounding the idea of being a mom and all it entails, losing the ability to have children should have been a small, if not nonexistent, blow. I was not the little girl who said she wanted to be a "mommy" when asked what she wanted to be when she grew up. I had never had the urge to procreate like so many of the women in my life. In fact, I spent a good portion of my life dodging the idea of parenthood like the last teammate on the losing side of dodgeball.

In my twenties, I quieted any maternal desires with a healthy mixture of pregnancy scares, trying to remember to take my birth control pills, hard liquor, and my annual plea that my OB/GYN tie my tubes because "I knew I didn't want children." Children were not in the cards for me. I had things I wanted to do; places I wanted to go. I wanted my life to be filled with romance and spontaneity, not screaming children and diaper genies.

And then I met Dan.

And without even noticing, my ideals did a complete one-eighty.

Well, some of them did. The drinking and smoking held steadfast.

Actually, let me rephrase, my ideals related to motherhood and procreation did a one-eighty. And, it wasn't because I hadn't had serious relationships in the past; I'd had several. But something about him (maybe it was the dimple) made my ovaries yearn for his baby. And sometime, early on in our relationship, the discussion about having children began to intermittently pepper our conversations.

(My apologies if this part triggers a gag reflex; even I can admit it's a bit much.)

"I know our children would be musically gifted," he'd say

with a smile.

"I wonder if she'll have a red afro," I'd retort.

"Hopefully he'll get my dimples."

While what I would consider a formal conversation never occurred, we still seemed to have come to the unspoken conclusion that we were going to be forever, and that children were going to have a starring role in our future.

Unfortunately, that specific dream, as I would soon learn, would be squashed under the heel of LAM as if it were nothing. I was only two or three appointments in after my diagnosis was confirmed (and hadn't yet made the trip to the NIH), when my doctor had "the talk" with Dan and me. There was a very large chance that pregnancy would accelerate my disease. And because of that, it was imperative we decide if that was a risk we were willing to take.

A lot of the quotes in this book are only recollections of what was possibly said. This is not one of those quotes. This is verbatim.

"If you are going to have children, you need to do it now."

There was not a smile in the room after those words were spoken. Nothing like death and pregnancy to spice up the honeymoon phase of a relationship.

I knew what Dan's answer would be. There is no way in hell he would risk my health so we could have a child. It was black and white for him. Without question. And yet for me, the girl who spent the better part of her adult life wishing away the thought of children, I didn't have it in me to give a definitive "no."

"It's not worth it," he said almost immediately after we had pulled out of the hospital. It's like he was inside my head.

He looked at me, knowing I was going to argue.

"Maybe it is," I said. I was shocked that the words had come out of my mouth so quickly. And sounded so angry. "I mean, there is a small chance everything would be fine. So, there is a chance we don't have to give up on this yet."

"No."

I could feel myself tear up at the sound of that word. It was so finite. So real. The thing I hadn't wanted until him was slipping out of my grasp. It was not a question. Not even the start of an open-ended discussion. Whether or not I had made my decision, he had made his. But I still had to ask.

"That's it?" I said between tears.

"You know this is the right decision."

I didn't. I had no idea what was right. What was wrong. I began thinking of all of the things I would never do; never experience if I gave up on the idea of children. I wondered if I would still be enough for Dan in ten years. In twenty?

Would he be enough for me?

Would I be viewed the same by my girlfriends and family?

I wondered what it looked like to grieve the loss of something you never had. What it looked like to cope (or not cope) with it. What I would say when people asked me why we didn't have children. (And they ask. Believe me, they ask. Always. Like it's their business because you're a woman and so are they, so the question is fair game.) The thought of another loss was exhausting, and the thought of trying to muddle through it simultaneously seemed impossible.

My brain had been so consumed with thoughts of LAM for the past year, I had not even had a chance to think about the ripple effect it would have. It wasn't enough to have a disease so rare that I had a better chance of getting struck by lightning. Twice. Now, more likely than not, I was going to be childless.

After years of wishing for that exact adult life, it had been taken away from me mere months after I'd decided that was what I wanted.

Touché, universe.

You truly are one vindictive bitch.

After NIH, I made the final decision.

Or rather they did. I just had no more excuses. No more reasons to wait just a couple more months for new or different information.

I just knew I could no longer justify my position even though I wanted to. My life for the life of my possible child? Absolutely. It was a no-brainer. Even with my fear of death, my desire to have and protect even the thought of my child surpassed all of those feelings. Funny, it seems I had maternal instincts after all.

Somewhere between returning from NIH and the New Year, I became ready to face my choice. I decided to blurt out my feelings one morning over breakfast; something that very rarely occurred in a formal setting. Pre-LAM, breakfast was black coffee and three cigarettes. Now it was usually a banana or undercooked English muffin. That day, we sat down and ate breakfast for real: eggs, bacon, and an excessive amount of hash browns. So, why not ruin a rare moment of Saturday morning adulting with discussions about our bleak and childless future?

"If we can't have kids, I want a permanent solution. I don't want a reminder. No daily pills, no IUD. I just want to be done."

Dan nodded. He had been waiting for me to make the decision he had made months ago, so I know he understood, even if I didn't.

And still don't.

* * * * * * *

My OB/GYN was a pleasant man in his early sixties who had come at the recommendation of one of my colleagues. I usually didn't put too much effort into finding an OB/GYN since they normally just rifle around your vagina and ask you how your parents are, but this one had to be special. I knew that upon our meeting, I had to ask him or her to sterilize me, and I needed someone who was going to understand my reason for the request. There is a large sense of vulnerability when a woman is sitting in a paper gown (that opens in the front) waiting for a man she doesn't know to walk into the room and examine her vagina. When he walked into the room, my mind was instantly put at ease. His presence made me feel like I could talk to him without judgement and, even though one would think it should be, that is not a trait that all doctors possess.

He sat next to me and asked me to tell him about myself. I dove into my diagnosis, no segue; my appointments over the last year; my trip to NIH. I explained that because of the estrogen theory, not only were kids not recommended, but neither was any birth control method that contained hormones. I told him that I needed a more permanent solution and I hoped he was willing to be the one to do it. My doctor at Vanderbilt had recommended tube removal; a full hysterectomy would not be ideal since that had the potential to dysregulate my estrogen.

"I just need to know what to do," I said.

He looked at me with kindness behind his eyes, with not one second of hesitation, and said, "If you were my daughter, I would tell her to do the same thing."

I wanted to hug him. So much of this had been so clinical and without emotion. This was one of the few times I felt myself—the person, the woman who would be childless—was being viewed in that light. I knew that I had made the right decision. This man didn't know me. He had no dog in this fight. And yet, he made sure I knew that I had his support. He'd found a way to make me feel less alone on my island, and I appreciated that more than he would ever know. He shook my hand and told me his staff would be in touch regarding scheduling.

* * * * * * *

I awoke from anesthesia with a sense of relief. I was less than two weeks out of my initial appointment and it was all almost over. Despite the tubal being my first surgery under anesthetic, the knowledge that the end was near overshadowed any slight fear I had of being put under. My eyes panned the room and were pleased to see the doctor in view. Much like he had during our first meeting, he sat next to me and smiled. But the smile was different this time. It was one that had an apology behind it instead of hope. I began to get nervous.

"We couldn't do it."

I'm sorry, what? Clearly, I was still heavily drugged out because there was no way I heard him right.

"We got in and there was a blockage. In any other situation we would have done a tubal, but with all of the cysts in your abdomen, I was just not comfortable. I'm so sorry."

Doctors apologize all the time, and for most of them it's an automatic reflex. This was not one of those times.

"It's okay," I said, attempting to offer him some comfort. I am aware of how strange that sounds, a patient comforting her surgeon, but I knew I wasn't the only person in the post-operative bay who was disappointed.

This meant none of this was over. I had resigned myself to the idea that on that day, I would no longer be a woman who could have children. Now, I still had the option. I had time to change my mind. I had time to picture my future with Dan and our son Edmund (his middle name) and our daughter Johanna (my grandmother's name). I could see all of us playing guitar like a modern day, interracial Von Trapp family. Those thoughts, which used to offer me happiness, were now dangerous. I had a future that was within my reach and yet absolutely unattainable. I was prepared to be sterile that day. I was not prepared to be given more time to second- (third-, fourth-, fifth-...) guess my decision.

Dan and I drove home in silence—an act that had quickly (and sadly) become a tradition. I thought about what my next steps would be. I knew that I needed to decide rapidly, and once I made the decision, I had to tell myself that I wouldn't change my mind. There was no way I was going to do what I did before and dwell on the choice to the point of insanity.

Regardless of my inner struggle, one thing was certain.

Dan was not going to change his mind. That was the only thing I seemed to know for sure. As he'd said before, my life was more important than something we weren't even sure was in the cards; a true testament to how much he loved me, yet one that was strangely heart-wrenching.

But I loved him. More than I'd love anyone before. That had to be the reasoning behind my decision; it couldn't rest solely in the hands of the "what if?" So, as my testament to him, only days after my failed attempt, I began making calls to see who would be willing to cut into my cyst-y abdomen and make me sterile. Within a week, I had an appointment at Vanderbilt with the oncology OB/GYN.

* * * * * * *

I sat in the cancer center at Vanderbilt and felt oddly at peace. While what I was suffering from was not classified as cancer, the other patients didn't know that. They smiled at me, gave me the sympathetic head nod, and it wasn't out of pity. It came from a place of understanding. It was the first time since my diagnosis that I didn't feel completely alone. A small part of me felt like an imposter, but the feeling of belonging I was finally experiencing seemed to negate any guilt I felt. And besides, from a technical standpoint, I had a foreign body multiplying in my lungs and destroying healthy tissue—sounded like cancer to me.

I was called back to the room by an overly pleasant nurse, a trait that was probably a prerequisite for working in this field and something I would normally find to be a bit much. In any other circumstances, her cheeky disposition would have grated on my last nerve, but in this instance, I found it strangely comforting. It was quite a change from the nurse practitioner, whose response to me saying I had LAM was "baaaaaahhh" (true fucking story).

Some doctors just look smart. Maybe smart is the wrong

word. Some doctors just look *brilliant*. And not in a collective like at the NIH, but on their own you can just tell they are going to be one of the smartest people you will ever meet. My new OB/GYN was one of those doctors. The kind of doctor who doesn't go home and watch Netflix, but the kind of doctor who goes home and does clinical research, or doesn't really go home at all.

She walked into the room, adjusted her slightly crooked wire-rimmed glasses, shook my hand, and sat down on her stool. I mentally prepared myself for having to give her a ten-minute explanation of my diagnosis, and why I wanted sterilization, and then having to explain that I had thought about it, and no I couldn't take birth control. Instead, she said this:

"I looked at your chart. You just want this part to be over, don't you?"

Holy shit.

There is no chance she didn't hear my sigh of relief. (The odds are also really good that I cried.) Finally, someone who got it. Someone who wasn't going to make me explain myself or feel bad, or ask me if I'd thought about other options.

"Yes, please," I said.

"Then let's get you taken care of."

About five more minutes were spent getting the logistics out of the way, and before I knew it I was heading home. In less than a month, I would officially be able to say I was unable to have children. I was naively optimistic that with this decision, reprieve would follow. At the time, I truly believed that if I was physically unable to have children, my brain would somehow stop thinking about it. I didn't even consider that, once again, I would be mourning a loss. It didn't cross my mind that I would feel like less of a woman because I was unable to reproduce. Or that I would scroll through social media and feel hatred towards pictures of pregnant women and newborns. And I certainly didn't think that I would feel guilty about forcing Dan to be with not only someone who was chronically ill, but also someone who was also barren.

It's been so many years since I could officially get pregnant that I almost don't remember what it felt like when pregnancy was something I talked about in the present tense. Some days I still want to travel back in time and slap twenty-something me in the face for being so flippant about pregnancy. If I was lying, this is the part where I would say that the idea of not being a parent has become a smaller pill to swallow. That "each day that passes is a day I think about having children less and less."

I could tell you, whoever "you" are, that the people who tell me "the grass isn't always greener" have a point. That when I smile and tell them they are probably right, I mean it. And I could pretend like I'm not that person who treats their dogs like children because they are overcompensating for a larger issue. Even if one of those statements was true, I'd consider that a win.

But not one of them is.

So, here is the most honest breakdown I can give. The rawest look into what it's like to be the woman who has to constantly decide how she wants to answer the question "Do you have kids?"

The things that, before now, I have barely even admitted to myself.

I think about children, *our* children, all of the time. Every. Goddam. Day. And I silently punish myself for the inability to do the one thing women are supposed to be able to do.

I feel lesser than. All the time.

I still yearn for a tiny voice to call me "Mom."

Despite my logical brain telling me otherwise, I still wonder if there is a good chance this is my punishment for terminating a pregnancy all those years ago.

I feel like I have nothing in common with some of my oldest friends because I am not a mother.

I still go home and cry after I hear someone say that "being a grandparent is the best gift of all" because I can never give my mom that gift. And I know she wants it.

I still feel like Dan resents me because I know how badly he wanted to be a father, despite the fact that he pretends otherwise. That I stopped being his soulmate, just a little bit, the minute I stopped being able to bear his children.

And that maybe he also stopped being mine. Just a little bit.

I will always wonder if my relationship with my mother will be slightly less important to her, because I am unable to make her a grandmother.

That I feel like I can't tell her I want her at my house for at least one Christmas every few years, because that's basically saying I think I'm more important than her grandchildren, which makes me a real asshole.

I'm sure there's more, but those are the major things. The things that live rent-free in my brain almost constantly.

So, in a true (and slightly cruel) twist of fate, I went from constantly thinking about not having children to constantly wishing that I did. And sadly, no matter how many vacations I take, or how many times people who have kids tell me it isn't always great, or how many times the medical part of my brain tells my heart that we made the right decision, I will always wonder if I made the right call.

There will always be fleeting thoughts of the "what if."

A lot of my thoughts about babies and motherhood are unfounded or uncertain, but one thing is true 100% of the time.

The emptiness is palpable.

CHAPTER NINE

The Dominican Republic

December, 2016

No babies? That means more vacations. At least, that was my thought process when I maxed out my credit card booking a romantic vacation at an all-inclusive resort in the Dominican Republic. I spent the following year planning the trip, and keeping it a secret from Dan so that it would be too late for him to back out by the time he knew about it.

If I believed in divine intervention, or karma, or "signs" or any other interjection from the universe, there is a good chance I never would have ended up in the Dominican Republic, drinking piña coladas, on the beach one day, and being rushed to the hospital in a 1986 Astro van the next.

But I didn't. Still don't. Even if I had noticed the signs, I was so blinded by making this vacation happen that there is a good chance I would not have paid them any attention. Frankly, it wouldn't have mattered if lightning struck our Uber on the way to the airport. I was going on this damn vacation.

I would repeat the following mantra to myself constantly: *If we can't have children, at least we can travel.* Parents don't get to be jet-setters unless they are Kardashians. But single people do.

So, travel we would. During my hiatus from work post-tubal, I went to a travel agent and booked us a Christmas trip to the beach, complete with a deluxe suite, unlimited drink package, and passes to multiple resorts. We were going to go cave diving, and swim with the dolphins, and do all of those things that people who are saddled down with children don't get to do.

Fuck it. I was gonna show them.

"Do you really think this is a good idea?" Dan asked, squashing my excitement almost immediately.

And just like in the movies, I responded with the one phrase that almost guarantees disaster. "What's the worst that could happen?"

On December 24th, the first "sign" arrived promptly at 3:57 a.m. (scheduled pick up was 3:30 a.m.) after our Uber driver had gotten lost on the streets of suburbia and called us twice for directions. He had GPS. And a cell phone. And a problem with women and brown people. Which should really be a category when someone is filling out their Uber profile. Do you like Bass Pro Shop and White Supremacy? If so, this is not the customer for you.

When he finally arrived, he was driving an old Caravan. You know, the kind with the faux wood panel along the side and the two rows of seats that could be removed in the most awkward and inconvenient manner possible. I hurriedly sat in the back seat so I wouldn't be expected to have a conversation with this guy, something I rapidly learned he wouldn't have done anyway since his talks with Dan included "not letting his woman touch the radio" and general racist rhetoric.

The trip to the airport seemed to take forever, despite only being fifteen minutes from our house, mostly due to the stench of stale Newports and sexism that lingered in the air. When we arrived at the departure gate, I retrieved my own suitcase out of the van (not that he would have offered), thanked him for the ride, and didn't look back.

"Well, *that* was interesting," Dan said.

"Better you than me," I said with a smirk.

Four in the morning was far too early for sexism, racism, or any other -ism he'd felt he needed to discuss with two total strangers. His four-star rating was lost on me.

The first portion of the trip was easy. Nashville to Charlotte in less than an hour. We had a two-hour layover, which would allow plenty of time for me to have enough drinks to sedate me enough that I could sleep for most of our three-and-a-half-hour flight to the Dominican.

The drinks happened. We boarded the plane. I drifted into a Billy-Joel-induced slumber. And then, everything began to fall spectacularly to pieces.

We'd been on the second leg of the trip for about two hours when the captain's voice came over the crackly loudspeaker. I had just started drifting off to the sounds of Billy Joel and I was annoyed at the poorly timed need for an announcement.

"So..."

He sounded like the boss from Office Space. At least that is how my memory has him sound.

"...we are having some mechanical issues that they can't fix in the Dominican, so we are going to have to turn the plane around. We're really sorry. We are heading back to Charlotte."

I was suddenly wide awake. I felt like a little kid who had been fighting with a sibling and her parents had decided to turn the car around and go back home. And what in hell was wrong with the plane that it couldn't be fixed at our destination? Or was it so severe that it couldn't make the rest of the flight that was already more than halfway over? This was not good. I couldn't even muster up the brain power to call the stewardess (sorry, flight attendant) over and make her bring me vodka. I felt Dan grip my hand tightly, and it almost instantly started sweating. I knew he was petrified, so we both just sat there, thinking at any time we were going to plummet to our deaths in the Atlantic Ocean. Sober.

This should have been sign numero dos.

Eventually, we made it back to Charlotte and I couldn't get off the plane fast enough. There was a bar conveniently located across the terminal so I could get good and drunk while the crew decided if our plane was "fixable."

Somewhere between the terminal and the bar (literally), Dan and I got into one of the hugest fights we have had to date.

"I told you we shouldn't have come," he said, his face getting red.

"And I said, I don't fucking care." And I didn't.

I tried to walk away but he followed me, his voice raised a few decibels. "We should just go home. This is a sign."

I spun around. "Really? A sign? Come on, Dan, you don't actually believe that. You just don't want to go." I flipped him the bird and headed towards the women's restroom so I could be sure he wouldn't follow me.

I'm pretty sure I told him to fuck off.

He threatened to go home instead of on vacation.

"I'll go without you. I don't need you there. I can sit on a beach and drink all day by my damn self."

People were looking in our direction, but I didn't care that we were "that couple." The ones who yelled and screamed at each other in public that I was normally ridiculing under my breath.

I angrily walked to the bathroom, while he headed towards the bar.

Eventually, in silence, we both found our way back to the terminal and sat next to each other like strangers. Without speaking, we had somehow agreed to get back on the plane together and attempt to enjoy our vacation. Like a true grudge holder (or more accurately, a grudge choker), I refused to speak first. I wondered how hard it would be to spend eight days on vacation with someone and not speak to them. I imagined with enough alcohol, anything was possible. I stuck my headphones in my ears, ordered a Jack Daniel's neat, and hoped that, despite being fueled by anger, I would be able to fall asleep. Perhaps waking up on the other side would allow me some perspective. It was Christmas, after all, and like all atheists, I wanted to celebrate accordingly.

This was supposed to be our getaway. Our trip that allowed us to, for a brief moment in time, forget the pungent dumpster fire that had been the last two years. The smallest bit of reprieve. So far, it had proved to be nothing but a mistake (something that I still refuse to admit). I drifted in and out of a shallow sleep while being sure to order several more dark-liquor drinks if the flight attendant was around and I happened to be awake.

I wished that I could start the morning all over again. A different Uber, maybe? Perhaps that was the key to the trip going well and I should have refused the musty driver and his K (for Klan) car.

Despite my stubbornness, somewhere mid-flight, our hands found each other, and I knew the fight was over. We didn't say anything, we just interlocked our fingers and simultaneously listened to our own separate playlists. Despite my propensity to hold a grudge, I knew it wasn't worth it in this particular situation. I mean, it was Christmas Eve, for fuck's sake. I squeezed his hand, looked at him, and smiled. He smiled back and I felt like I could relax just a little bit. The hard part was almost over.

Not. So. Much.

* * * * * * *

The airport in the Dominican Republic looked like the line for an amusement park ride that had just opened. Despite my original plan to be half drunk on a beach by this time, we stood in a line with hundreds of other passengers who were also waiting for the same thing. I looked at my watch (not true, I don't have a watch, but that sounds better than "I looked at my iPhone") and noted that it was 9:00 p.m. We had officially been traveling for eighteen hours and I could not have been more over it.

Remain calm, I thought. We are almost there. At one point, two dark-skinned gentlemen offered to pull me out of line and allow me to skip the waiting. I was ready to abandon all reason and follow them to whatever lay beyond the never-ending sea of people; however, Dan seemed to think that would have caused us to end up on an episode of *Dateline*.

Wuss.

I am sure it was no more than an hour by the time we were in our shuttle being driven to the resort, but it felt like days. All I wanted to do was check in, get to our room, and fall into a deep, uninterrupted sleep. Tomorrow morning was Christmas, and I intended on spending the day with a consistent buzz in one of my new maxi dresses. Just as God intended.

The resort was beautiful. I could tell, even in the dark, that this was going to be money well spent. We were handed a glass of champagne while we were checked in and it wasn't five minutes before we were driven to our suite, which was complete with an indoor hot tub, private balcony, and most importantly, access to a minibar. Our butler...

(yes, a butler a la Tim Curry in *Clue*, but less murder-y)

...introduced himself and let us know he would be back in the morning and would meet with us to go over our options for the next week.

It wasn't long before both our heads hit the pillow and sleep was not far behind. Tomorrow was going to mark the start of a wonderful week.

* * * * * * *

Christmas Day.

I awoke a few minutes before Dan and walked out to the balcony. The turquoise ocean was visible in the distance and I could hear the waves crashing on the shore. The air was salty with just a slight breeze and zero humidity, which my lungs and black-girl hair both appreciated. The space between our room and the beach was lined with palm trees, and our balcony overlooked the pool and swim-up bar. It was exactly how I had envisioned things when I booked the trip.

Relaxation. Sex. Romance. And of course, the obligatory, "don't you wish you were us" selfie. This trip was going to be the perfect way to reset—I found myself experiencing effortless happiness for the first time since December 2nd. Maybe, despite the difficulties leading up to this moment, this would be what finally catapulted me out of my miserable, self-absorbed, previous two years. I had spent that time in a horrible headspace and found it hard to think about anything other than LAM. It was time to pull myself out of my funk with the assistance of Jose Cuervo, my man Jack Daniels, and countless pretty pink drinks with umbrellas in them.

By the time Dan joined me, and we had spent a good amount of time enjoying the calm, we realized we had slept in too long for breakfast. Our "butler" ...

(note: I am using quotes because I am uncomfortable with using that terminology, but that was how they described themselves. Concierge would have been more appropriate...but, as usual, I digress)

...recommended we grab lunch at the one sports bar on the resort; appropriately named "Sport Bar." Singular. I had been to Mexico with some girlfriends a few years prior and I had a fond memory of the fresh fruit that lined the breakfast buffet. I was craving pineapple in particular, but just for today, a hamburger and fries from "Sport Bar" would have to do. I could have all the fresh fruit I wanted tomorrow.

We spent our lunch laughing at inside jokes and the fact that the same song played on repeat for the duration of our meal. The anger from yesterday had been completely forgotten, mostly likely due to a combination of Dos Equis and sheer exhaustion, but it was gone, nonetheless. The beach was within our grasp as well as all the fruity drinks I could stomach. We each had one more drink before grabbing our towels and heading to the beach via our own personal golf cart.

The water was clear and even bluer up close, and the beach was covered in white sand. We quickly found two lounge chairs and almost instantly, my much-sought-after fruity beach drink was delivered. I managed to muster up enough courage to get about waist deep in the ocean, despite my crippling fear of sharks, in order to capture a picture of us in the ocean wearing Santa hats. I had every intention of posting the finished product to social media to make everyone home jealous as they spent their Christmas in thirty-something degree weather eating a ham. Because ham is the fucking worst.

The picture I had so badly coveted would become much more visible than I had originally intended.

The beach was followed by a swim in the pool outside our room and a quick nap before we headed to dinner. We ate faux Italian food in a dimly lit room. In most circumstances, I would have bitched and made a flippant comment on the mediocrity of Italian food, but on that night, it was more delicious and satisfying than any Italian food I had ever eaten (apologies to my very Italian uncle).

I could picture the next eight days, the food, the ocean (viewed from the beach, of course), and hopefully the sex on expensive white linen sheets. For the first time in an extremely long time, my smile was involuntary. I was with the love of my life at a romantic resort for the holidays. I felt untouchable.

And to top it all off, my unpronounceable lung disease was safely tucked away in the recesses of my mind, roughly 1,500 miles in my periphery.

Sleep found us early and easily that night. Maybe because of our ability to finally relax, maybe it was the distant sound of the waves hitting the shore like nature's metronome, or maybe (most likely) it was because neither of us wanted to miss the breakfast buffet two days in a row. Regardless, it was the best I'd slept, and felt, in two years. So far, this trip was worth every single penny. All 60,000 of them.

That was the last fond memory I would have of our trip. Everything after that was a nightmare.

* * * * * * *

As I opened my eyes the following morning, I was greeted by sunlight streaming across the white comforter and a digital clock that read 6:55 a.m.

I don't think so.

While I was excited to get a start to the day, I knew I had a good couple of hours before I even had to concern myself with waking up and looking presentable. I stole a quick glance at my sleeping boyfriend and drifted back off to sleep, thoughts of fresh pineapple and ocean-side strawberry daiquiris lulling me into a slumber.

When I awoke the second time, Dan was already awake and showering in preparation for our well-deserved tropical breakfast. After wiping the tired from my eyes, I sat up and stretched. Almost immediately, I felt a brief but painful twinge in my chest.

At first, as crazy as it sounds now, the thought of something medical...

(I say something medical like I wasn't aware I had a fucking LUNG issue, and that the sensation felt exactly like a lung collapse I'd already had, and like I wasn't a goddamn nurse)

...being the cause of the pain didn't even cross my mind. I mean, I'd made it two years without an issue and, in my head, the odds of everything going to shit the week I was on the vacation of my dreams were slim to none. I shook off the brief "twinge" and decided to make my way out of bed to shower and get ready for the day. I stood up and was almost instantly knocked back by the sharp discomfort I felt in the center of my chest. It was as if someone had whacked me directly in my sternum. With an ax.

There was a short-lived moment where the pain did not register, and I simply felt stunned.

It was, however, fleeting, and the agony quickly followed.

No way, I thought. Clearly, I was still in a state of denial driven solely by euphoria and mild insanity. *This is not happening. I am just overreacting. Get dressed and go get some goddamned pineapple.*

I attempted to walk the short six-foot distance from the bed to my suitcase and immediately began coughing. I sat back down on the opposite side of the bed, thinking that a moment of rest would cure what was, most certainly, a moment of bodily inconvenience. As I sat and attempted to grab hold of my bearings, my mind involuntarily traveled back to the day I sat in that meeting, coughing uncontrollably and feeling generally "blah."

Not today, lungs. Please not today.

I stood again and attempted once more to walk towards the other side of the room. A shower would have to occur later; if I could just get dressed, maybe this would all go away.

No dice.

Despite my willpower and desire for a normal vacation, the pain had become constant and almost reached a debilitating state. I sat down on the side of the bed and waited for Dan to finish showering. I wanted to let him enjoy the last few minutes of the vacation he could barely be convinced to go on in the first place. (Not only that, but there was no way I could have reached the bathroom even if I wanted to.) I could feel the tears welling up in my eyes. Not just because of the pain, but because of an additional mix of fear, frustration, and guilt.

We'd only had one day. One. Fucking. Day.

Panic mode began to set in. Strangely, it was not in the sense of a medical panic, but more of the dread I felt surrounding the relationship concerns that would surely result if what I thought was happening was actually happening. I had literally begged, on multiple occasions, to have Dan set aside his (what I believed to be) irrational fear of the worst-case scenario and allow us to just be. I booked the trip without even consulting him because I knew that it wouldn't happen if he had had a say in the matter.

I truly believed that I knew better.

If my lung collapsed in a developing nation, how on earth could I fix the lasting effects of that event on my future with Dan? In what way could I possibly begin to repair the damage caused by the exact medical emergency Dan had promised we would face, but that I had promised him was as improbable as a UFO sighting? If he was right, and I was wrong, would we survive?

And then, I had a thought.

An inter-monologue Hail Mary, if you will.

I bet I can fake it. I bet I can pretend like I feel fine. Time to put all of those acting skills to the ultimate test.

Get your shit together, Sara.

Take the deepest breath you can and act your ass off.

Hell, I could make it a few more days with a collapsed lung. I just had to concentrate on the bigger picture. And, if I could just make it a few more days, then at least I could rationalize the money spent and, more importantly, I could blame the collapse on a coincidence as opposed to the trip itself.

Despite my will to believe the ultimate smoke screen was possible, I grossly underestimated my significant other's ability to read me like a Danielle Steel novel. Shortly after my failed attempt at regularity, I was reminded of the reason I both adored him, and, in a brief moment of irrationality, resented him.

Dan came out of the bathroom and without him saying a word, I know that he knew exactly what was happening to me. He'd spent nine months telling me he thought traveling that far was a mistake, and I'd told him time and time again that I would be fine and he was overreacting. In that moment, he was kind enough to not utter the words "I told you so" (or maybe he just didn't think to) before he dove across the bed and attempted to call the butler (concierge).

I choose not to question his reaction. Instead, I decided to assert my independence. Because why not.

"I can walk downstairs," I said, but he was already halfway out the door by the time I got the words out of my mouth.

He returned minutes later with the kind-eyed butler...

(Okay, I'm going to stop correcting the job title simply for the sake of political correctness or American privilege. You know my feelings about it.)

...who helped me walk down the stairs and into a golf cart. I could feel my breath becoming increasingly labored, even after I was safely in a golf cart on my way to the resort urgent care. The first office was closed, something I found odd considering it was past 9:00 a.m. at this point and considering the size of the resort. I was removed from the cart at the request of the driver and escorted to a small standalone building on the outskirts of the resort. I sat in the dingy waiting room while our driver checked to see where the medical staff was. It felt like an eternity before he was ushering me back to the golf cart and driving me to the second location.

In that moment, I had a new and much more morose epiphany.

Fuck. I was going to die here.

And, from the looks of it, I wasn't even going to get to die with our beautiful suite as the backdrop. Or in my sleep. Instead, I was going to lose my life in what could only be described as some oubliette in a corner of the resort no one goes to, while Dan tried to decipher what was going on, using his broken Spanish because neither of us had thought to download a translation app.

There were medical professionals who spoke fluent English who didn't understand my diagnosis, so I figured my chances of survival were minimal at best. And it was no one's fault. Okay, that's not entirely true. It would be 100% my fault.

After waiting outside in the once breezy air that had somehow become stale and heavy, the decision was made to drive me across the resort to the other medical facility. Thankfully, the second location was open, although I was unclear what life-saving interventions would be available at any location on the resort. The golf cart was parked and we were taken into a small room where we were greeted by a short blonde woman. Before she could ask any questions, I attempted to explain to her that I couldn't breathe; that I had a rare disease; that I needed to go to a hospital.

Her English was broken at best, and my Spanish was nonexistent. I had no clue how I was going to explain the severity of the situation. I could tell she wanted to help; she wanted so badly to understand, yet my ethnocentric brain was annoyed at the breakdown in communication.

Instead of doing *literally* anything else, I did that thing where I just repeated American words at a louder decibel, thinking that eventually, the sheer volume of my voice would result in her understanding. I cursed my rare disease. I cursed my mother's insistence that I take Latin in high school instead of a language that would allow me to communicate with a population other than dead Romans. Eventually, in a series of hand gestures I can only credit to my theater and/or charades experience, I was able to explain that I was having severe respiratory issues. After what felt like several lifetimes, she looked at me, smiled, and said, "Asthma?"

Without me having to insult her with any additional Neanderthal-like hand gestures, she placed a pulse oximeter on my finger. Almost simultaneously, her smile was gone and the color was drained from her face. I stole a quick glance at the oximeter.

It read 84%. If that's your grade on a test, you're not doing too badly. If that's your oxygen saturation, you're close to failing at life. For comparison, an oxygen saturation of less than 88% is considered dangerous, with an oxygen saturation of below 85% warranting a trip to a hospital. Less than 80% can be fatal; a level I was teetering on without further intervention.

Dead. In the Dominican Republic.

She swiftly placed me on oxygen and went back to the front desk. Dan followed closely behind so he could arrange an ambulance, but not before he looked at me and said,

"I think it's time you called your mother."

I didn't even try to argue. I picked up my cell phone and took as deep a breath as I could. This would be all of my years of drama club put to the test. I could not freak out, because I knew *she* was going to freak out. I had to pretend like everything that was happening was no big deal.

"How's your trip?" she asked after she picked up. "I'm so glad you called. I was wondering if I would hear from you."

She sounded so happy. Relieved, almost. "It's good, Mom." I choked back the tears and started talking again before she could get any further. "Well, I mean except for one thing." I paused again.

Jesus, Sara, just get the words out before you physically can't. "My lung collapsed."

She didn't say a word.

"But I'm fine," I lied. "Dan is working out the ambulance right now. I'm fine though, I promise."

I wondered how many times I could say the words "I'm fine" before the words ceased to have any meaning.

Two?

Three?

Seventy-four?

She barely choked out the words "I love you" before abruptly hanging up the phone. I knew her well enough to know that meant she was going to cry and didn't want me to hear it. I wished I could have stayed on the phone and had her voice in my ear until things calmed down, but if she was crying, I would cry, and that would not have been good for anyone.

At some point, Dan had paid the random ambulance fee that was apparently not included in the $6,000 we spent on the five-star resort. (All-inclusive, my mocha-colored ass.) Shortly after, I was being walked to the ambulance (Astro van) to head to the hospital. Nine months of planning. My savings account was drained. My paid time off that I had meticulously hoarded was in a negative balance. And now, instead of hoping the trip would never end, I was trying to figure out how on earth I was going to get the fuck out of the Dominican alive.

CHAPTER TEN

The Death Chapter

Even as I begin to put these words down, I can feel my chest getting heavy and a lump welling up in my throat. I'd say we are looking at a minimum of ten panic attacks prior to completion. I probably should have taken a Xanax...or five.

I had some time to think about things on the ride from the resort to the hospital, and I only thought about one. Dying. It wasn't a new thought; I had always had fleeting ideas of death and the finality of it all, but for the first time in a long time, the thought was constant.

As a child, I had what I would now call an unhealthy fear of dying. I know I thought about it more than most kids—to the point where I was obsessed with not only the death of people around me, but my own death as well. I have a clear picture of lying next to my grandmother in bed while she was trying to put me down for a nap, and sobbing uncontrollably because I didn't want her to die.

Dramatic from the get-go, it would seem.

The fear became relentless and it eventually morphed into one thought: that once I died, I was dead forever, a word that quickly became terrifying to think about. It would keep me up at night and occupy almost all of my thoughts during the day. I was that kid who wanted to live forever, not because I thought immortality was cool, but because I was petrified of the alternative.

Fast forward thirty-ish years.

Most adults I know have no desire to live forever. The older we get, the more we are supposed to accept death as an inevitability and eventually, come to a place where we will almost welcome it when it arrives. And yet, for me that fear is still present. Even before my diagnosis, it was a constant nagging thought that took up residence in the back of my brain. And while it wasn't my focus like it was when I was a kid, it was still always present.

I don't want to die.

Even when I'm old.

At one point, not that long into my official diagnosis, I went into a full panic. I locked myself in the tiny half bathroom off of our bedroom, called my mother, and could barely get the words "I. Don't. Want. To. Die." out of my mouth before I completely lost my shit and ugly cried on the bathroom floor.

How childish.

And selfish.

And completely thoughtless.

But I didn't care. It didn't matter to me that my mother was most likely hurting more than I was. That she was already feeling helpless, and frustrated, sad, and scared that she may outlive one of her children. I didn't care. I wanted my "mommy" and I wanted her to tell me, just like she would have when I was a kid, that my death was long off and it was nothing to worry about.

"You won't even know," she would say.

I don't remember now what her response was. Most likely that I wasn't going to die, just like she would have told me thirty years before. Only now, I knew that she didn't believe it anymore. Or maybe she believed it, just not 100%. I imagine it's much easier to tell a six-year-old in perfect health that they shouldn't be concerned about dying than your daughter who, for all intents and purposes, may in fact die before she is supposed to.

Being an adult brought a new caveat to the fear: atheism. The dread of dying is different for an atheist. Death is not only imminent, but it is final. As a child, I wasn't sure about the forever part because I still had God in my life. Sure, it scared me, but heaven was my safety net. Now, there is no reincarnation, no hell, no purgatory, and certainly no heaven. Death just is. And when it happens, that's it. It's not meant to be melancholy, just factual (or at least what I believe is fact). And the fear goes beyond the finality. I worry that I won't be ready. I'm absolutely petrified that when that day comes, I won't be in a place where I have accepted death.

And that level of terror is palpable.

I've had thirty-plus years to learn about death and deal with it, and yet, somehow, I am that same scared six-year-old kid who cries at the thought of her funeral.

Seems healthy.

Moving on.

Death certainly isn't unique to a rare diagnosis. There are plenty of illnesses that make people rethink their lives, and contemplate death and what it means. Cancer is one of those illnesses. Sadly, I know far too many people who have been diagnosed, some who have sadly lost their battle, and some who have beaten the fucker like a champion. This is where the difference between becomes evident.

Cancer is beatable.

And did you know that when you complete chemotherapy, sometimes you get to ring a bell? I didn't.

Ringing the bell signifies that you have completed your treatment and have essentially slayed the cancerous dragon. I imagine it is one of the best feelings in the world to be lucky enough to walk towards and ring that bell after what I'm sure is months or years of feeling like you were living life on a battlefield.

You ring the bell. And then, the best part. You get to say the three words that I would think every single cancer patient is waiting to say since the day of their diagnosis: "I beat cancer."

Three words that are universally followed with praise, prayers, hugs, and testaments to the strength of the individual who fought Goliath. And won.

As it should be.

Let me say those words again before I continue.

As. It. SHOULD. Be.

As a disclaimer, I debated putting this section in at all because I am well aware of how this could be received. And rightly so. But I swore I would be blatantly honest, even to the point of sounding like a horrible person. So, I'm going to say it. Out loud. For the first time. (After a deep breath and a shot or two of Jack Daniel's.)

I wish I had cancer.

Not in the Munchausen Syndrome way. Believe me, I have no desire for people to view me as a sick person. But if I had to pick between LAM and cancer, I would pick cancer. I've often wondered if I am the only patient who feels this way, but my fear of judgement has stopped me from asking the question.

Cancer is scary, but it is also a known monster. When you say, "I have cancer," people don't look at you with a blank stare and make you explain, for the umpteenth time, the logistics of your diagnosis and how it slowly kills whatever organ it has decided to take residence in. When you say, "I have cancer," people understand the battle that is about to be entered and they are more than willing to suit up and march with you.

Cancer is a shark.

LAM is the Loch Ness monster.

It's not to say that I haven't had the best group of people rally around me, but it's different. I didn't believe that recognition of a disease would make any sort of difference, but it does. Cancer universally sucks without question. LAM sucks, but only to the people who know it. And sometimes that's okay. But sometimes I wish LAM was a diagnosis universally acknowledged.

But back to the bell.

Sure, I'd love it if people knew what LAM was or if they didn't make sheep noises when I said it (I know I mentioned that story before, but it really does bear repeating). But that isn't the real issue. For a while I thought it was, but it wasn't until I learned about that bell that I realized why I really felt the way I did.

I want to ring that fucking bell.

Or hit a gong.

Or blow a bugle.

Or even "ping" a triangle.

I want to say I "beat" LAM.

And that is one thing I will never get to do. It's like some weird version of Groundhog's Day where I suit up, fight the battle, win the war, and then wake up the next day only to do it all over again with no hope of resolution. It's maddening. And exhausting. Worse yet, I don't know how to articulate it to the people I love in a way that doesn't make me sound like I'm slowly descending into madness.

Two of the women in my family were diagnosed with breast cancer at roughly the same time I was diagnosed with LAM. They lost their hair. They underwent multiple surgeries. They had chemo that put them out of commission for days at a time because of the shitty side effects. They were unable to hold their newborn babies. And they remained graceful and poised through the entire ordeal.

And then?

They both beat it. They both kicked cancer's ass (as they say) and it was amazing to watch.

And I was jealous.

Then I felt like an asshole because I was jealous.

Then I felt alone because I couldn't tell anyone that I was jealous.

Instead, I would let the feelings brew inside of me until I randomly lashed out at Dan.

(Still do, but hopefully not as often.)

I so badly wanted to be able to wake up one day and tell the world that I kicked LAM's ass. That I finally won my battle. To be able to utter the words: "I am LAM-free."

But I can't. And most days, I am not okay with that, but I still pretend that I am. And I pretend that I don't spend 90% of my day stewing about the disease that is eating away at my ability to breathe. And I pretend that I'm not the mentally deranged person who is jealous of people with cancer. And I pretend like my life is exactly the same as it was. And I pretend that I don't have LAM.

But I do.

And there is no cure.

No chemo.

No magic weapon.

No goddamn bell.

Now, let me be clear about something. My fucked-up feelings about my diagnosis and death do not change the fact that I am going to do my best to fight more often than not. Some days, I find it harder to do than others and, in the interest of full disclosure, there are many days I don't fight at all. I do my best to be strong. But I can't pretend that it wouldn't be a bit easier to take if I knew there was a possible victory down the road.

Even though my death and my diagnosis leave me feeling alone even when I'm not, a good friend once told me something that has stuck with me through it all. That summed it up so perfectly.

"Everyone intermittently questions their mortality. But yours rides with you in the passenger seat."

Yup. That's it. In a perfectly macabre nutshell.

CHAPTER ELEVEN

El Hospital

There was mold on the wall.

The image of black fungus crawling up the back wall of the triage room was the first thing I saw as I was wheeled into the ER. There is some sort of irony to the idea of breathing in black mold with a collapsed lung and, despite the circumstances, I chuckled to myself. The ambulance (and by ambulance, I mean the 1985 Astro van) drivers didn't speak as they left the room. Not that my six years of Latin would have helped me understand them (thanks, Mom), but it would have been a nice gesture. The table I was placed on sat directly under a drip in the ceiling that conveniently hit my bare leg as it fell. I counted the drips in an effort to keep my mind occupied.

One.

Two.

Three.

Four.

Five.

Six...

Dan had been called out of the room for some reason and the sound of silence was only broken by the drips.

Seven.

Eight.

Nine.

My mind wandered as my eyes scanned my surroundings. My imagination was not deterred by my inability to breathe and I began to think of the dozens of horror films that take place in hospitals. The overall look of the hospitals in these movies is the same. A hospital that, despite being fully staffed and treating patients, looks dilapidated and haunted. The halls are dark, the lights flicker, and the doctors and nurses look much more menacing than compassionate. I always wondered who the patients were in these hospitals and figured if they were killed by a crazed ax murderer, they deserved it for agreeing to be admitted to such a disturbing place.

This was *that* hospital.

At least in my head it was.

The sense of sterility one normally feels when they enter a hospital was replaced with a feeling of "don't move and don't touch anything." There was a small window to my left with a view of some sort of tropical tree. I would later learn that I should have been more thankful for the limited view, as the neighborhood that hospital was in had been described by Dan as "less than ideal." (Actually, it had been described as "ground zero in a developing nation" but that's neither here nor there.) The room was large and mostly empty.

I sat in silence and hoped that all this was a fluke. Some sort of rare heartburn that only comes from eating the Dominican version of Italian food. Or even better, just a vivid nightmare that would quickly end with me waking up in a sun-soaked room on white 1,000 count sheets with only the sound of the ocean in the background.

It wasn't too long before someone was in the room taking vital signs and asking questions in Spanish. Dan followed quickly behind and sat in the only chair in the room. They figured out quickly that I didn't speak the language and communicated from that point on by smiles and nods. Somehow, they obtained the information they needed and afterward, I was taken by the hand and led to what I could only assume would be my chest x-ray.

I wanted to demand that Dan come with me—the thought of being left without him gave me a feeling of dread I had never experienced before. As I opened my mouth to request that he accompany me, I realized almost simultaneously that making demands in a language no one else understands is the very definition of a moot point. And a really gross American. Without giving it a second thought, I allowed them to lead me down the hall to the radiology suite with Dan sitting alone in the moldy room.

I have seen (and heard) some very strange things in hospitals, especially during the years I worked as a nurse on a locked psychiatric unit. What was behind the radiology door was a first: two men with spackle, open paint cans, and tools strewn about met me on the other side of the door. Some words were exchanged in Spanish and the two men exited, leaving their mess behind.

Mold. Check.

Lead-based paint. Check.

Collapsed lung. Check.

My lungs were having a field day.

The x-ray went quickly (thankfully) and I was returned to the triage room to be with Dan.

We sat in silence, both on our phones updating everyone in the U.S. with the state of things and trying to be sure we responded to each text that seemed to be coming through at an unimaginable rate. At some point, the door opened and a short woman with brown hair entered carrying what I could only assume was a chest tube tray.

"Hello," she said. Her English was limited but understandable, which was a welcome surprise.

I smiled at her and waited for her to tell me what I already knew.

You have a small left-sided pneumothorax which will require a small chest tube and should resolve in twenty-four to forty-eight hours.

Not. Fucking. Quite.

"It's your whole lung," she said, matter-of-factly.

"Excuse me?" I couldn't stop the tears from coming at that point, but somehow my brain stopped me from yelling *"What in the actual fuck?"*

This was a far cry from the first collapse that, while life-altering, was so small it would not have shown up on a simple chest x-ray. Apparently, the years had erased how that first collapse felt or I would have known this one was different. That initial punch to the chest feeling and my inability to walk meant things were far worse. In a true worst-case scenario event, I was four hours into a total left-sided lung collapse in a foreign country, where there was mold on the walls.

No way this was real. Any of it. This had to be a night terror.

"It's the entire left lung," she repeated. "You'll need a chest tube."

Without thinking before the words came out of my mouth, something that seemed to be happening constantly that day, I looked at her and said, "I want to go back to America."

I realize now how pretentious that sounded, but apparently, when my lung collapsed, my filter had shat the bed along with it.

Without missing a beat, she replied. "If you get on a plane now, you will die." Not in a cruel way, but just very matter-of-fact.

And that wasn't it. She went on to explain that I would receive no further treatment, to include the insertion of a chest tube that was certainly the apparatus that was going to keep me alive, until I paid the hospital. She would be back after the money was received (not a moment sooner) and with that, left the room, leaving the chest tube tray on the counter before she closed the door behind her. I looked at Dan, who was still managing to keep his game face on. I started doing a tally in my head. Room and board, plus chest tube, plus anesthesia (do they even *have* anesthesia), plus ER charges...

It didn't really matter what the total amount was, we didn't have it. My credit card was at its max and, due to my crippling shoe addiction, my checking account was lackluster at best. I looked over at Dan, who was feverishly texting who I can only assume was my mother.

She doesn't have it either, I thought as I cursed myself for not making more rich friends as an adult.

The only other hospital staff member who spoke even a little bit of English was a beautiful woman who had long dark hair, a kind smile, and was about eight months pregnant. She entered the room, said a broken hello, and handed me a piece of paper facedown. I slowly turned it over, like the recipient of a piece of paper with a dollar amount on it always does.

$8,7--

I stopped reading. I didn't know anyone who had nine-hundred dollars just lying around, let alone nine *thousand*. I felt like I was going to be sick(er). I should have made it a point in my early adult life to surround myself with friends who were filthy rich.

But hindsight is...well...hindsight.

There I sat, one piece of shit lung, and a "bill" that was preventing me from getting any sort of relief. I looked longingly at the chest tube kit that sat by the sink and wondered if I'd seen enough *Grey's Anatomy* to perform the procedure on myself.

Dan took my hand. "I'll take care of it, baby," he said without missing a beat.

In a normal situation I would have asked how. I would have wanted a plan for a probable that seemed impossible to solve. I would have told him that I didn't want to ask anyone for that amount of money. But this was not a normal situation. We were so far from normal that any everyday solution was not going to cut it. So instead, I just squeezed his hand and watched him follow the pretty pregnant woman out of the room.

It is hard to say now how much time passed before Dan was back. I am not even sure there was a clock in the room. The strange thing is, I wasn't losing track of time because I was scared, which I really should have been. I was sitting in a hospital in a developing nation, my left lung was totally collapsed, I couldn't breathe, I was on no pain meds, and I was being refused treatment. By all accounts, I should have been in full-blown panic mode. However, something in my brain was stopping me from completely losing my shit and I was beyond appreciative. I was losing track of time because my brain seemed to have completely shut down all other functionality in order to focus on keeping me alive.

Worked for me. Sheer panic had no place in my current situation.

Eventually, Dan came back, staring at his phone with a strange look on his face. I wondered how long he would wait to tell me that we couldn't get the money. I wanted to scream at him to blurt it out and get it over with. As the woman at the resort told me, I could live with one lung.

"You have a GoFundMe account," he said without looking up from his phone. "And it's already at $10,000."

If I hadn't been already short a lung, that statement would have taken my breath away.

$10,000, I thought. *That's insane.*

I didn't need to ask who had started it. I knew better. I had three overzealous friends who I would later find out had not only started the campaign, but had also been on the phone with my specialist at Vanderbilt and called the U.S. Embassy—twice. When the offer for a GoFundMe had been presented to me in the past to assist with my mounting medical bills, my pride had not allowed me to agree to it. I had a sneaking suspicion the culprits knew I could not contest it in my current state. I made a mental note to yell at them when I was back in the U.S.

"People seem to really care about you," he said with a grin. The first smile he had been able to muster all day.

"Or they just feel guilty," I said without missing a beat. Apparently, I had lost my filter, but it seemed my cynicism was still intact. Good to know.

He didn't respond, just squeezed my hand and then left the room, likely to find someone to finally shove a tube into my chest. I sat on the table, mindlessly scrolling through my phone in an effort to keep my mind focused on the inane postings on Facebook, and not counting the seconds that seemed to be passing at a snail's pace. Eventually, Dan and the pretty pregnant woman came back in the room. Her demeanor had changed from stoic and business-like to pleasant and comforting.

"Your credit card payment was accepted," she said with a smile. Apparently $9,000 bought you treatment as well as bedside manner.

Knowing I would ask, Dan turned to me and said, "Your grandma's credit card."

I guess you don't need a rich friend when you have a frugal grandmother.

Almost simultaneously, the surgeon was back in the room. What she said next, in any other circumstances, would have put me at ease. I'd like that she felt a bit guilty for the refusal of treatment and was doing her best to "make it up to me."

"You need a fairly large tube. We are going to put you under."

I felt a lump rise in my throat and my mind began to race. I had done well keeping the dark thoughts at bay until that point, but the thought of being pumped full of the Michael Jackson drug in a country where I did not speak the language was more than I could take.

What if the drug was dangerous?
What if it wasn't even a real drug?
What if I had a reaction?

What if I didn't wake up?

The last thought lingered like the smell of stale beer the day after a keg party.

There was a good possibility that the last thing I would ever see was Dan's face fading into the background as I was wheeled down a hall lined with mold. I am sure I could have declined. I could have said that I wanted a bottle of whiskey and a belt to bite on and been done with it. I'm not sure if it was the language barrier or my fatigue catching up to me, but I just didn't have it in me to tell them that being unconscious was the last thing I wanted.

At some point amidst my internal panic, Dan leaned in and kissed me on the forehead. We did not share a verbal exchange, just an unspoken second or two of mutual understanding. The moment I had pictured in my head was real now. His face, the only familiarity I had, slowly faded away as I was taken to the operating suite.

I was parked in a hallway facing the doors to the OR suite. I peered through the smudged windows into what looked to me like a cross between medical supply storage and a morgue.

How appropriate.

The orderly left me in the dimly lit vestibule (let's say the lights were flickering too, for effect) and disappeared without a word. I listened to my surgeon and a large black man, who I can only assume was the anesthesiologist, discuss something in Spanish. I hoped it was my case and how well it was going to go, but there was no way of knowing. I tried to close my eyes and wander off into thoughts of where I was supposed to be: sitting with the love of my life on a beach, drinking far too many fruity drinks with straws in them. I attempted to forget about the moldy walls, the staff who couldn't understand me, and the idea that I may never wake up from whatever they were going to do to me in the OR.

It took the little bit of energy I had left to make sure I didn't allow any tears to come. If I *was* going to die in this tiny OR, I was not going to be crying when it happened. And despite my belief (or lack thereof) in the afterlife, if I was wrong about it, I was certainly not going to spend my first day in heaven with bloodshot eyes and running mascara. Just before my mind went to a place that was too dark, the anesthesiologist came out to wheel me into the OR. He looked at me with his kind eyes and smiled.

"It will be okay," he said, as if he had been spending the twenty minutes inside my head.

I closed my eyes and concentrated on the sound of the squeaky gurney wheel as I rolled out of the vestibule and into the OR.

* * * * * * *

The sounds of an agonizing groan woke me out of my anesthesia-induced sleep.

I was awake. I knew I wasn't out of the woods, but at least I was awake. I slowly opened my eyes and attempted to take in my surroundings. To my right, a window. The broken blinds were pulled down, so there was no view of the outside, but I remember being grateful for the idea of only being separated from the outside by a window.

I have no clue if I had been in the OR for minutes or hours; when I ask Dan, he usually tells me he's not sure of the number of hours, only that it felt like forever.

To my left, the source of the groan. A curtain was the only thing separating me from the patient who sounded as if every pained breath was their last. I was not sure if I was in ICU or postop—or if a postop ward even existed. I shifted in bed and felt the pull of something on my left side. I could only assume it was the chest tube that suddenly felt like a garden hose jammed into my rib cage. Hell, there was a good chance it was an actual garden hose.

I turned back to my right and noticed Dan sitting below the window with the broken blinds. There is a good chance he had been there the whole time, but I didn't notice him until now. He looked up from his phone and smiled. Without asking for permission, likely because he knew the answer would be a resounding "hell no," he snapped a photo of me, which I could only assume was my most unflattering to date. (It was and still is.)

"Everyone needs to know you are okay."

I knew Dan well enough to know that by everyone, he was including himself. I wanted to reassure him and tell him that I was fine; that I was out of the woods; that I was going to be okay. But I didn't have the heart to lie to him, and I certainly didn't know if it was true. Sure, I was out of surgery, but there was still so much unknown in front of me. I had no clue how long I would be here or how long they would need to treat me, or with what. The only thing I knew was that I wanted to go home. All I cared about was getting someone to understand that I needed to go home. Now. Or before now.

A staff member suddenly appeared, I assumed to check my status.

"Time to go," she said in a thick accent.

I looked at her in shock.

What is she talking about? Home? Did a miracle happen? Was I going to be able to leave?

She pointed towards the window at Dan, who was feverishly texting and didn't initially notice that her statement was directed at him.

This had to be a mistake. There was no way she was talking to Dan. I knew the rules of an ICU. I knew that I was allowed to have someone stay with me, especially if I protested. More importantly, I was not in a mental state where I should have been or needed to be left alone. There was no way I could spend a night alone in this hospital and not lose my fucking shit. As Dan stood up to head towards the door, I took his hand, silently begging him to stay.

I needed to talk to someone; to explain to a staff member

that Dan leaving wasn't an option. That he'd behave himself and just sleep quietly through the night. Unfortunately, having an argument with someone who doesn't speak the same language is like pissing into the wind. So, I cried. Spanish tears. Ugly Spanish tears.

Certainly, that would cause her to reconsider.

She didn't. I got nothing. Not even a sliver of empathy.

When she didn't react, I tried to stop the tears, which only made it worse. I was doing that cry that was accompanied with equal parts snot and hyperventilation. Dan squeezed my hand, placed a soft kiss on my forehead, and without another word, he walked past the rows of beds and out of the ICU ward. I was defeated. All the fight I had left was out of me. I wanted to pull out my IV and chest tube and run after him. I wanted to go to the airport and get on the first plane back to the States.

I rolled over onto the side that was chest-tube free and stared at the window. I looked at the broken blinds and imagined what was on the other side. At some point, I fell asleep. It was most likely a combination of whatever medication I was on and the extreme exhaustion that had finally taken over. I was done for the day. I was done trying to force myself to be strong; to make my brain go somewhere else; to actively distract myself from thinking I was going to die in a hospital where chickens were running around outside.

Tomorrow, I would panic.

Tonight, I would sleep.

* * * * * * *

I woke up in the morning to an overzealous nurse who decided I needed a vigorous bed bath, even though I attempted several times to tell her I was all set. It was quite the change from the eight-by-eight tile shower that sat empty in my suite across the island. I had a new appreciation for all of the patients I had had to give bed baths to during my tenure as a nurse. I felt exposed. Degraded. Dirty. Dirtier than I would have felt had she just let me stew in my own filth. It wasn't just the bed bath. It was the bath coupled with the fact that if I'd told her to stop, she would have just looked at me, smiled, and kept right on putting her washcloth places I didn't want it to go.

I realized that, at some point during the night, my groaning neighbor had been silenced. I hoped it was because of medication and not due to the alternative, but it was hard to say. It sounds awful, especially as a nurse, but I did not have the energy or empathy in me to worry about someone else's shitty luck. Other than that, the light of day had changed nothing about the dreary ICU. I closed my eyes, hoping that some lingering exhaustion would somehow allow me to sleep through the humiliation of lying naked while being sponged by strangers; sadly, it did not and that memory will always remain.

Eventually, the most awkward bath of all time (so far) was over and I could go back to only worrying about how I was going to get home with one good lung. The nurse draped a paper gown over me and threw the used washcloths into a bin of water. She gathered her things and turned to leave. Before I could even take a breath, she turned back around.

"Panties?" she asked, holding up my underwear.

She must have seen the look of confusion on my face. Actually, it was likely a look of confusion *and* disgust, as "panties" is one of my least favorite words in the English language.

She clarified. "I take panties."

Almost no one spoke a word of English, but goddamn, they knew the word "panties" and apparently, they also knew its ability to make my skin crawl.

Before I could protest, she was gone, my underwear clutched in her hand. I could only assume her plan was to wash them. Or sell them on the black market. Not only that, but now I was clothed only in a paper gown, with no bra, and no...

Panties.

Shudders

I never did get the underwear back. And yes, I still think about it all the time.

I sat in my bed, barely clothed and naked from the waist down. This day was not starting off well although one could argue it was going better than the previous one. I panned the room for a clock. It was the first time since I had arrived at the hospital that I cared what time it was. Somewhere between awake and asleep, someone had told me my visitor could come back at noon.

Almost like she was entering her scene in a play, a familiar face appeared from behind the curtain. It wasn't Dan, but it was the next best thing.

"Good morning, Sara," my surgeon said with a smile.

She walked towards me and I realized that I never asked her name, and likewise she had never offered it. Despite our brief meeting the previous day, her voice, her face, and her smile offered comfort like an old friend.

"You look good," she lied.

She stood at my bedside examining what I am sure was a gaping hole in the side of my chest.

She took my hand. "You can move."

For a fleeting moment, I thought maybe she meant countries, but I quickly dismissed the ludicrous thought. I was moving out of ICU. While I didn't relish the fact of spending another night without Dan, the ICU had quickly become familiar and the thought of any more change was almost more unbearable than the chest tube. Without another word, she was gone, disappearing behind the curtain.

* * * * * * *

My new room was (thankfully) unoccupied. While my anxiety level was still at a solid eleven, it did put my mind somewhat at ease that for the time being, I would not have to share my room, college dorm style, with a patient who probably had some highly contagious disease. The look of the room was reminiscent of the type of motel where the desk clerk is standing behind bulletproof glass. The good news was that unlike the ICU, Dan was allowed to stay the night. In retrospect, it was extremely selfish of me to expect him to stay in a 1980s hospital bed when there was a perfectly good suite awaiting him at the resort. But I just couldn't bring myself to tell him he could go. The thought of one more night without him made me physically ill.

With my new room came a new accessory. The tube coming out of my chest was attached to what could only be described as a growler (or a jug, for those of you who aren't seasoned drinkers) that had about two inches of water in the bottom. It was secured to a metal IV pole with duct tape, so I was at least able to walk back and forth to the surprisingly modern bathroom. I took my phone and snapped a quick photo to send to my doctor; and for posterity, of course. She had been a source of calm throughout the ordeal by letting me text her consistently to keep her updated.

It looks like their version of water seal, she texted back. *It's how it used to be done and perfectly safe.*

"I'm going to keep making calls," Dan said as he stood facing the window.

At some point amidst the chaos, he had vigilantly started the process of trying to get me back to the States. There was no way to know how many calls he had already made at that point, but I had no doubt he had been going nonstop since that morning. To add to the financial punch to the gut we had taken yesterday, my insurance company had signed a new contract with a medical transportation company that stated a patient could be transferred from anywhere in the world to any covered facility without paying out of pocket—starting the first of the year. Four days away.

Of fucking course.

Without insurance coverage, my flight home would be roughly $32,000. Suddenly, the $8,000 and change my family had dished out to the hospital seemed like peanuts.

I grabbed the remote and tried to find some mindless show to watch that wasn't in Spanish while Dan paced around the room and the hallway, trying to figure out how we were going to get me home. The health care professional in me knew that it was virtually impossible to have a medical flight put in place by the end of the day. The patient in me knew that I couldn't possibly spend another night in this hospital with no sense of when and how I was going to get to go home. Even with Dan by my side, I could feel myself starting to lose what little positivity I had left. I needed something definite to hold on to. Just grasping on to hope wasn't going to cut it for much longer.

It was nearly 5:00 p.m. when we finally got our answer. I had been intermittently drifting in and out of sleep while watching an obscure comedy I had found on TBS.

"Pack your bags, we're out of here tomorrow."

Before I could ask him how on earth he had moved mountains to get me home, he told me that he had been on the phone nonstop with the medical flight company to the point he and the representative were on a first name basis. The two of them had worked tirelessly to get a crew to me so that I could finally be transferred to the States.

"Thank you." I wanted to say more, but I didn't.

I should have been excited, but the word 'tomorrow' hung in the room like a stale odor. Dan could obviously sense my disappointment, although there is a good chance he didn't have to sense anything and my feelings were written all over my face. He came over and sat next to me on the bed.

"You can do this. You can. This is the end, and it's just one more night." He kissed my cheek and looked at me with his grey/blue eyes. "You've. Got. This."

I smiled at him, swept his hair off of his forehead, but said nothing. I was afraid if I opened my mouth to speak, the ugly cry would happen again and that wouldn't do anyone any good. Twenty-four hours had never seemed so far in the future. I silently wished that the fluid in my IV bag was laced with a high-dose sleep aid that would allow me to fall into a coma-like state and wake up in a hospital bed in Nashville.

CHAPTER TWELVE

The Plane

The staff of my medical flight walked into my room wearing flight suits. Legitimate, one piece, navy jumpers.

I'm also not entirely convinced they weren't walking in slow motion like they were an R&B group in an early 2000s rap video.

A tall black man with long dreads, think Busta Rhymes circa 1998, led the pack and spoke first. I found his presence comforting, despite his large and brooding stature.

"You must be Sara," he said with a grin. I don't think I had ever been happier to hear someone speak English in my entire life. (Yes. I am aware that sounds extremely ethnocentric. Judge me if you must.)

Dan walked over to him and shook his hand. They exchanged pleasantries and all the while I was thinking, *The quicker you end this conversation, the quicker I can get out of here.* There were two nurses in tow, one sporting the above-mentioned flight suit and the other in what I could only describe as pediatric scrubs. My nurse friends will understand that reference, but for those of you who don't, picture bunnies or baby duckies. I would later learn that she was training and I would be her first flight. I knew I didn't have room to talk considering my current living conditions, but part of me wished I hadn't been "stuck" with a trainee. Especially if she was going to slow things down.

"Is this your chest tube container?" the non-training nurse asked, pointing to my fluid-filled growler.

"That would be it," I said. "It seems to be doing the trick, despite appearances."

"Well, no offense, but I think we are going to go ahead and switch it out for ours."

"I'll allow it," I said with a grin. Frankly, they could have switched it out for an old wine bottle and I would have let them if it meant I was closer to getting home.

While they exchanged my container for an actual chest tube drainage system, I wondered if I should take the old one with me. The methods of the Dominican hospital, while somewhat archaic by first world standards, as well as my own, were still methods they had used to attempt to save my life (after a small $9,000 fee). For that I was grateful. I decided against asking for the souvenir, thinking it may have been viewed as mockery or as an insult to their practices, while my intent would have been to keep it as a reminder that as long as the method saves your life, who gives a shit what it looks like. Since I did not have the energy to explain my desire to keep the growler, it would stay in the Dominican and hopefully have the chance to save someone else.

While I tried not to wince from the pain of changing the apparatus, Dan gathered the few belongings we had brought to the hospital and followed me, my flight staff, and my new container out of the room. Our luggage would be enjoying the rest of our vacation at the resort until other arrangements, if any, could be made to get it back home. It would not join us on the plane due to weight restrictions, which did not put my already nervous mind at ease about the size and stability of the plane.

Once again, Dan and I would have to split up until we got to the airport. I would ride in the back of the ambulance while he would take a cab and be forced to go through customs, since our arrival in Nashville would not allow that on the backend. I crossed my fingers and hoped that nothing else went wrong and I wouldn't be forced to be on a puddle jumper with the tube in my chest as my only familiar companion.

Clearly, my overly tired brain was operating on a "worst-case scenario" basis by that point in time and could only imagine the experience as a negative one. While I was once again preoccupied with my own thoughts, Dan kissed me goodbye at the double door and turned to leave as I was loaded into the ambulance. I took a glimpse, my last, of the vacation I had fought so hard for, and of which I had only experienced a small taste.

I watched the leaves of a palm tree sway slowly back and forth in the almost nonexistent breeze. I took a deep breath in before they closed the doors to the ambulance and we headed down the highway towards the airport. Dan would later tell me that the best thing that ever happened to me was that I didn't see the neighborhood where the hospital was located. Based on the condition of the hospital, I believed him 110%.

The ambulance pulled onto the tarmac in an isolated section of the airport. The door opened and, with the assistance of the staff, I stepped off the gurney and walked up the four or five steps that led me to my next and final mode of transportation. The inside of the plane looked like it used to be a rich person's travel companion. Plush leather chairs lined the plane with the exception of the several that had obviously been removed to leave room for a gurney. The plane was likely the tiniest I had ever flown on and yet, somehow, in this tiny puddle jumper I felt the safest I had in the last two days.

I made some small talk with the respiratory therapist, who luckily seemed to have the same sarcastic sense of humor as I did. He and the non-trainee nurse bantered back and forth and laughed together, which set my mind even more at ease. A stoic demeanor in the medical field was something I didn't practice as a nurse, and it was certainly something I didn't appreciate as a patient. Give me all of your jokes and all of your dark humor, and I'll be good to go.

The nurse trainee was a different story. She was clearly nervous and looked as if she was going to be sick, from one or both ends. On top of that, she had a cough that would have made a tuberculosis patient blush. After her tenth or eleventh time hacking into a tissue, the seasoned nurse asked about her very obvious illness.

Without explanation of what exact disease she was battling, she responded with, "My husband mentioned I may not want to come..."

Cough, cough. Phlegm. Cough.

"...but I told him I would be okay."

Nearly hacks up lung.

I silently giggled at the irony of the situation. Here I was, a single tube keeping my lung inflated long enough to get home (hopefully), a hole in my chest, about to be in yet another pressurized air situation, and my nurse had some sort of respiratory plague. Most times, I value a good work ethic, but, in this instance, I would have preferred that she train with someone who wasn't already one lung down.

Just let it go. You're almost home. Breathe.

It seemed like we waited for years before I finally saw Dan's head poke through the plane door. In that moment, I was finally, 100% convinced that we would not be separated again. It was a level of relief that I hadn't experienced in two days and it felt like a boulder had been lifted off my chest, despite my current pulmonary condition. He grabbed my hand as he walked to the back of the plane towards a small bench that was tucked away in a corner. I silently wished that Nurse Typhoid would have given up her seat so I could be closer to him (and away from her respiratory shrapnel), but at least he was there.

I told him he needed to lie down and sleep. He nodded in agreement, although we both knew rest would not come easily on this flight. We both shared a crippling fear of flying, him slightly more so than I. I would find out after the fact that just before we left for the trip, he'd had a horrible nightmare in which a plane, much like the one we were on, crashed. Had I known that then, I would have realized how condescending it sounded for me to tell him to rest. And perhaps I wouldn't have fought so hard to make him come.

I adjusted myself on the plane's small gurney and looked out the tiny window to my left. Despite my phobia, I remained at ease knowing that, sans plane crash, I would be touching down on the Nashville Airport tarmac in a little over four hours.

Dan placed his hat over his face and curled up on the bench the staff had turned into a bed for him. A bit more small talk ensued and then, almost without warning, we were in the air. At that moment, I decided that if I ever won the lottery, my first purchase would be a private jet. There was certainly something to be said for not waiting for people to slowly pick their seat, for not being forced to sit next to a crying baby or a chatty Cathy, or waiting for some pretentious prick to fit his barely eligible suitcase into the overhead bin (because there is always one of those). That being said, the chances of Dan ever getting on another plane with me were probably less than my chances of being diagnosed with LAM in the first place, but it was nice to have my mind wander to a happier place than it had been in the past forty-eight hours.

I spent a majority of the flight staring out the window at the clouds. Normally, I made it a point to sit as far away from the window as possible so I could pretend I was on a bus as opposed to being hurled through the air in a giant steel tube. For some reason, on this tiny plane where normally I would be sick to my stomach with worry, I had found a sense of calm in watching each cloud pass by. The only thing missing was my go-to Billy Joel flight playlist which, sadly, was back with my luggage enjoying a king-sized bed and a minibar. Thank God (you know, the one I don't believe in) for the clouds.

The cabin of the plane was mostly silent for a majority of the trip, with the exception of a random cough from the sick nurse. Eventually, the sight of the ocean disappeared from view and the plane was finally flying over land. Only a little while longer. The end was so close.

On the last leg, I turned away from the window and noticed that my favorite nurse was missing from her chair. I suddenly recalled that the captain had said something about turbulent weather. I could only assume she was crying in the bathroom, most likely what I would be doing if I wasn't strapped to a bed. Well, that and if I wasn't still amid my newfound (and eerie) sense of calm. As the turbulence started, I closed my eyes and thought of how good it was going to feel when the wheels touched down in Nashville.

We landed in Nashville around 8:00 p.m. on Wednesday, December 28th. The nurse trainee remained in the bathroom (it turns out her stomach wasn't made for small planes or turbulence) as the rest of us shuffled out of the plane. As she opened the door a crack to slip her passport through, I could only assume that the bathroom looked like she had eaten a bad clam in Santa Clarita; not to mention how bad it must have smelled. Dan yelled out a quick thank you to her through the crack in the door before following us off the plane.

The rest of the team would be accompanying me to my room at the hospital, which was a good thing; I felt strangely tied to them and was not ready to have them leave my side. Despite the fact that I had only known them for about six hours, they felt like old friends and that warranted a proper goodbye, not just a wave from the back of the ambulance.

The cold air felt amazing on my face. It couldn't have been more than forty degrees outside, and Dan and I still donned our vacation garb; he in his cargo shorts and me in an unwashed maxi dress with NO PANTIES (gag). He gave me a quick good-bye kiss, an act that had become very commonplace the last few days, and walked towards the black town car that had been sent for him. As I was wheeled towards the last ambulance that sat waiting for me in the dark, I took a look at my surroundings. We were in an isolated part of the airport that I could only assume was where all of the rich people landed their private jets. It was cold, secluded, and black. And yet, I felt an overwhelming sense of euphoria. Most times, getting back to the airport is the worst part of a tropical vacation, but I can say, even now, that it was the best part of the entire trip. I was finally nearing the end of an ordeal that I still couldn't believe I had experienced.

As the ambulance drove out of the airport and towards the hospital that was awaiting my arrival, I took in a deep breath. It was painful but felt amazing at the same time. I was driving not only towards treatment, but also towards my mom, who had arrived in Nashville from New York in record time, and towards my friends. The glorious humans who literally paid my way.

Fuck, I was home. I was safe. The end was close.

This is almost over, I thought. *Things can finally go back to normal.*

Unfortunately, my ordeal was far from over. My tropical lung collapse had put into action a series of events that would keep me out of commission for another six months. While I cannot say I am thankful for what the ordeal taught me— because let's be honest, that would be total bullshit—what I am thankful for is that I was blissfully unaware of how much worse things were going to get before they got better.

CHAPTER THIRTEEN

The Long Stay
December 2016 and January 2017

I am going to get medical-ly for a minute. Nurse or otherwise, when people get diagnosed with anything out of the ordinary, they become experts in that field. Most times this is not on purpose, it is just a side-effect of attempting to be informed. One of the scarier things I learned about was called a pleurodesis, a procedure that I didn't even know was medically possible until I had been diagnosed.

> *Pleurodesis is a procedure that is designed to get the two layers of the lung lining (the pleura) to stick together. This works to obliterate the space between the layers (the pleural cavity) so that fluid (water, blood, or pus) can no longer build up between the layers. (www.thelamfoundation.org)*

How does that work? I'm glad you asked.

> *In a pleurodesis, a chemical (talc) is injected between the two pleural layers via a chest tube. These chemicals then cause inflammation, which in turn causes*

scarring. This scarring pulls and holds the two membranes together so that fluid or air can no longer build up and collect in the space.

Surgical pleurodesis may be performed via thoracotomy or thoracoscopy. This involves mechanically irritating the parietal pleura, often with a rough pad. Moreover, surgical removal of parietal pleura is an effective way of achieving stable pleurodesis.

While neither sounds like a walk in the park, the talc procedure (a doctor literally puts talc into your chest tube, which serves as a sort of cement) sounded slightly less horrid than the mechanical. Unfortunately, talc was contraindicated (fancy medical speak for not a good fucking idea) because of the possibility of lung transplant down the road. It would seem that the talc makes it more difficult for your lung to be removed due to the adhesion process. Mechanical pleurodesis is the preferred treatment for recurring pneumothorax in LAM patients. A fact that can *easily* be found if you simply google "LAM pleurodesis." (This is an extremely important piece of information to remember for later.)

There was no question that this was what was waiting for me over the next couple of days. I knew enough to know that one collapse equals chest tube and then home. Two collapses mean surgery (now you get it after the first collapse), with the hope that would ensure my lung would behave itself. My insurance did not allow me to be treated at Vanderbilt, which would have been ideal considering my specialist was there, but I was sure that whoever was treating me would take the proper steps to ensure everything went the way it was supposed to.

Mistake #1.

(Of many.)

I know a lot of doctors. When you spend over ten years working in the medical field, it only makes sense that a number of doctors will cross your path. And I loved them. For all of their quirks, idiosyncrasies, savant-like intelligence, and their genuine love for all they do. The internal medicine docs, the OB/GYNs, the urologists, the pediatricians (who randomly liked to be called by their first names), the psychiatrists (who could sometimes be confused as psych patients themselves), and even the ever so arrogant surgeons all had their very own way of showing they gave a real shit about their patients.

Maybe I was just lucky, but 99% of the time I respected them, admired their intelligence, and legitimately enjoyed their company.

I met my pulmonologist the evening I was admitted. I was hoping that my chipper young doctor from two years before would be showing her face, but no such luck. This doctor was a tall slender man who, despite a kind smile, did not share my propensity for sarcasm. While his bedside manner left a little to be desired, I found him to be compassionate and accommodating. He allowed me to speak my piece and agreed to call my doctor at Vanderbilt, a request most doctors found condescending coming from their patient. But my gut told me that he understood, and while my request may have been a blow to his ego, he didn't let it show.

He excused himself after a plethora of questions from myself and my mother and told me to get some rest. It would be the best night of sleep I would have for the foreseeable future. I'm not sure if it was all of the new pain medications, my exhaustion, or a calming combination of both, but that night I slipped into the most glorious nocturnal coma of all time.

When I met my surgeon on December 29th, I was still flying high on the euphoria of being in a hospital with no mold, no leaks, and where I understood what everyone was saying. His arrogance did nothing to deter my faith in him.

Now, brace yourself. You're about to meet the 1%.

Most surgeons are arrogant.

Most surgeons have a God complex.

Most surgeons have traits that are deal breakers in forming a friendship, but that I absolutely require in a doctor, especially one who is going to be rooting around inside my chest cavity. This surgeon was no different. Not at first. He was curt and confident, and I had no reason to question him. I know now that if I had not been neck-deep in a trauma haze, I would have made sure I asked the questions that should be asked before someone operates on your already broken lung.

Do you know about LAM?
Did you call my specialist?
How many of these procedures have you done?
How long will the procedure take?
What should I expect after the procedure is performed?
What is the recovery time?
Are you a douche bag?

If I had had the wherewithal to ask even one of those questions, I know his response would have caused me pause. Because he hadn't called my specialist. And if I had to guess, he had probably only done a handful of the procedures that I needed done, and he *certainly* hadn't done any research on my disease. Also, I am pretty sure he would have said "yes" if I'd had the chance to ask if he was a douche bag. Proudly.

All of these issues were going to become glaringly obvious, but only after he had already performed the surgery.

Mistake #2.

* * * * * * *

I awoke from my surgery groggy and hopeful. The hard part was most certainly over and now I could begin to heal, not only from the surgery, but also from the entire ordeal. I knew my story from a LAM perspective was far from over, but I was certainly ready to be finished with this particular chapter. I enjoyed the comfort of the remnants of the anesthesia while I drifted in and out of sleep. My mother sat quietly in the corner knitting, most likely for my new nephew who had been born a month before. While many of the days of this experience are groggy and opiate-laden, this next portion sticks out like I would as the guest speaker at a Klan rally.

Somewhere between naps, Angie had shown up to visit. Something that is important to know about Angie is her complete lack of boundaries when it comes to her friends. I know it's okay to write this because it is something she admits to herself. Her overwhelming and unconscious need to stand up for her friends, no matter the status of the person who she believed had wronged them, would play an important role in the next series of events.

"How are you feeling?" she said as she entered the room. "Any pain?"

"No." I smiled at her so she knew I was telling the truth.

"Pain meds still doing their thing. Lucky you."

She pulled up a chair next to my bed, snapped some photos for an article I wasn't sure I'd agreed to be in, and made herself comfortable.

Somewhere in the midst of all the small talk, and the jokes about how amazing my vacation was, whatever was left of my preoperative pain medication wore off. Now, I am going to do my best to describe the pain in a way that translates, but I dare say it was close to indescribable. It felt like, out of nowhere, someone had plunged a dull knife into my abdomen, and was just slowly twisting it back and forth. It was a pain that caused me to lose the ability to speak, not an easy feat, ask anyone; it caused my heart to race; it caused my teeth to clench; it caused tears to fall without warning and almost instantly. Angie and my mother rushed to my bedside and hit the call button without me even having to attempt to ask (which I couldn't have done anyway).

A nurse I didn't recognize entered my room, and I was convinced she'd walked there from Calcutta. Familiarity was not my concern, so I didn't much care that I hadn't seen her before. I just needed her to inject something in my IV bag that would make the alien baby trying to birth itself out of my stomach stop.

"You're in a little pain," she said with a smile.

I wanted to throat punch her.

"She needs her meds. Now." Angie wasn't playing games, and I couldn't have been more grateful.

The nurse walked over to the computer and she typed my patient information into the keyboard one miserable peck at a time.

"I'm going to have to get your nurse," she said, as if I should have known that was going to be her response.

"I'm sorry, but why?" I was reaching a boiling point with this woman.

"Oh sweetie, you're not due."

This woman was lucky I was being held down by pain. Not only was she denying me pain medication, but she called me sweetie. It was like she had a death wish.

"I got my last dose at 9:00 a.m.," I said between tears. I mustered up my last bit of patience to do some quick and really fucking simple math. "It's every four hours and it's 2:30. I know I'm due."

Despite the clear anguish on my face, she continued to smile. (I can't make this next part up, and both Angie and my mother can attest to it.) She looked down at her hands and began to count the hours on her nubby little fingers while mouthing each hour under her breath.

Ten.

Eleven.

Twelve.

One.

Two.

Two-thirty.

"Oh well, then I guess you are."

Another fucking giggle.

She left the room and I exhaled deeply.

"You'll be fine, I promise." Somewhere in the midst of my pain, Angie was standing next to me and my mother was on the other side, each tightly squeezing a hand. One of them said those words and I know what that meant, no matter which one said it. Get this girl medication, or heads will roll.

My chipper yet math-challenged nurse eventually sauntered back in with my pain medication: a two mg dose of morphine. I was nothing if not an expert on the effects of morphine at this point, and I knew there was no way this was going to put a dent in my pain level. Going from a ten to a nine was not going to cut it.

"There's got to be something else?" It came out as a question, but it was meant to sound more like a demand.

"This will take care of it," she replied.

Oh, fuck all the way off.

My nursing brain kicked in and I realized quickly what had happened. My surgeon, in all his egotistical wisdom, had spent the morning poking around my chest cavity and decided that did not warrant an increase in the amount of medication I might require. Not to mention, there was still a goddamn tube lodged in my side. Even a rookie would know that postoperative medications need to be stronger than preoperative medications. Not only is it a standard of care, but it's a kindness that most doctors should exhibit: anticipate that the patient will be much more uncomfortable after their procedure, especially one that was literally performed to be an irritant to an already sensitive area.

I looked over to Angie for solace and she was feverishly texting someone. She looked up at me and responded almost as if she had read my mind.

Queue the rolling heads.

"I'm getting in touch with Dr. Young. This is friggin' (she may have said fucking) unacceptable."

Normally, I would tell her that it wasn't Dr. Young's problem and that we could figure it out, and that we had bothered her enough on her vacation, but I truly didn't care. If she had to text the Pope himself, I was good with it as long as it meant whatever I was feeling would stop. Dr. Young responded as if I was her only patient and she was waiting for any text or call regarding my care. I believe the phrase "feels like childbirth without medications" was used, but I cannot be sure if that is what she said or just how I felt. Angie walked over to the white board and wrote Dr. Young's instructions down.

"I've got to go," she squeezed my hand one more time, "but this is exactly what they need to do. And if they don't, let me know."

"I'll take care of it." Uh oh. My mother had entered the chat. And she was officially pissed. This would not bode well for anyone in the wake of her wrath, but it would certainly benefit me.

I stared at the myriad of medications and instructions that Angie had received from Dr. Young and wondered how any one of us was going to go about telling a doctor that we didn't think he was doing his job. Especially this one. He didn't exactly present himself as someone who wanted to be told they did something wrong. Ever.

I closed my eyes and tried to tell myself I should be grateful. Grateful I was alive, grateful there was no mold on the walls, grateful my mother was by my side. Instead, I was angry at the nurse who couldn't figure out simple math, I was angry at the surgeon who assumed my postoperative pain would be minimal, and once again, I was angry at my janky lung for causing all of the issues in the first place.

Eventually, it's hard to say how long it actually was, but it felt English-Patient long, my pulmonologist walked into the room. Certainly, he would understand. He could easily look at the expression on my face and see that I wasn't full of shit. Or overacting. Instead he said this:

"I mean, I'm not sure that the pain medications needed to be changed, not to mention the surgeon is really in charge of prescribing postop pain medications."

Oh sir, you just made a huge mistake.

Just as a thought, my mother was not having it. She had reached the end of her rope and her mama bear instincts had kicked in.

"You will give my daughter every single mediation written on that white board. This is unacceptable."

That's how you make a demand, I thought. Get 'em, Mom.

The doctor was taken aback. If he was a cartoon he would have made a doctor-shaped hole in the wall as he ran out of the room. It was clear he wanted to spew more excuses, but instead he just said, "I'll see what I can do."

He left the room and I wasn't entirely sure I would see him again, but it wasn't thirty minutes later that I was being gifted with a PCA Pump, a bag full of pain medications with a little green button you can push every thirty minutes to an hour to give you the relief you need. The button glowed like a beacon, and I had never been so happy to press a button in my life.

Turns out, that bag was filled with Dilaudid and if you have never experienced Dilaudid, you are missing out. Not in a "you should use it recreationally" kind of way, but in a "if you are in severe pain, there is nothing like it" kind of way. The first dose washed over my body like a warm bubble bath and the pain relief was immediate. Or should I say, my level of not giving a shit about the pain was immediate? Either way, I closed my eyes, thanked the nurse in a slurred voice, and almost immediately fell asleep.

It's all going to be okay.

The days began to blend together after that. I only knew what time of day it was by who was visiting. My mother always arrived at 9:00 a.m. on the dot and Dan showed up to relieve her in the afternoon between 4:00 p.m. and 5:00 p.m. Sometimes they brought food, sometimes they brought stories of what was going on around me while I was confined to a bed, and sometimes they just sat with me and begrudgingly watched an episode of *My 600-lb. Life* that I had certainly already seen.

"Goodnight, baby," Dan would say right before he kissed my forehead and left me alone for the night.

"I love you."

Each night, the door would close behind him and I knew it was going to be another long and lonely twelve hours.

The only real difference between the days and nights I was in the hospital was that at night, there were some nights I was all alone. Every so often, I got assigned to a night nurse who would use any down time he may have had to come sit with me when I couldn't sleep. We would gossip and laugh and talk about life. He provided me a calmness that could only come from someone who wasn't directly involved in the situation. I longed for his shifts and even more so, the nights that were slow so that he could spend as much time with me as I needed.

Take note, nurses: this is the stuff that sticks with your patients.

After the surgery, day after day came and went and my lung, for some reason, would not stay inflated. As a result, I was hooked to something called wall suction for days at a time. What is that, you ask? Well, it's high-octane fun for all ages.

In the most basic of descriptions, your chest tube is hooked up to a vacuum in the wall, which means you can only travel as far as your chest tube will allow you to. And, for the love of all things holy, don't try to go further. No amount of Dilaudid will fix the pain of a chest tube being stretched past its limit.

* * * * * * *

Two and a half weeks passed; I had been sitting in the hospital for seventeen days and nothing had changed. I rang in New Year's in a party hat a friend had dropped off, sitting alone in a hospital bed watching a *Snapped* marathon. I had played countless games of Solitaire, Phase 10, and Two Dots. And, much to my mother's protesting, I had watched every episode of *Snapped* at least once. I had washed myself using only a towel and a basin at least ten times, and at other times my mother was forced to bathe me, an act of love, I know, but it was also the only bath that was more awkward than the pant-ie-raid washing I'd had in the Dominican. I had experienced nightly 3:00 a.m. chest x-rays, and I hadn't taken a shit in two weeks (the one downside to my Dilaudid joy).

This was not how I envisioned things going. This was supposed to be the part where I got better. Where I got a quick surgery and then was sent home to recoup in my own bed, with my own food, and my very cuddly new puppy. Unfortunately, despite the hose in my chest, and the surgery I was assured did "exactly what it was supposed to," I continued to sit in the hospital. For some reason, my lung still refused to stay inflated. Every time a step was taken to attempt to wean me off of the chest tube, my lung, in protest, decided to deflate (a feat that earned my left lung the nickname Tom Brady).

Early in the morning on the seventeenth day, I got a visit from the case management director. A visit from case management usually means a discharge is being planned. Had my lung finally behaved? Was I going to get to go home?

The answer to both of those questions was a resounding "no."

"They are going to transfer you to Vanderbilt."

I wasn't sure what to say. I didn't want to go to yet another hospital, I wanted to go home. I wanted to throw a tantrum right then and there. I wanted to hold my breath and stomp my feet. I wanted to hide in a corner and curse the world. But instead, I just nodded and let her explain the process.

"The transfer can happen at any time. We won't know until they call. If a bed opens at midnight in three days, then that's when you will go."

More uncertainty. Just what I wanted. If I was going to stay in a hospital, I wanted to stay put. I had become accustomed to the nurses, and the techs, and the cable, and the private room. My brain told me that a transfer was the right thing if I ever wanted to put an end to this drama, but my emotions told me that I couldn't handle starting over yet again. I thanked the case manager, and she left the room saying she would keep me posted as best she could (which meant not at all).

I swear. I am not making this next part up. No one was there to witness it, but I promise it was not the drugs. This. Actually. Happened.

Shortly after the case manager left, in walked my surgeon.

In scrubs (appropriate).

And cowboy boots (a little strange but it *is* Nashville).

And a leather vest (no words).

I should have kicked him out then and there for his crimes against fashion that did nothing but exaggerate his overall doucheyness. Instead, I wondered silently to myself if he actually thought he looked good or if he had lost a bet.

"The procedure didn't work," he said without as much as a good morning.

What was your first clue?

"We are going to do a talc pleurodesis. Today." It was not a question.

Wait, what? I had been told I was being transferred. I had been told I'd be treated at Vanderbilt. I had been told I couldn't have talc because of LAM. What in the actual fuck was happening?

With a click of his man-heels, he left the room.

Mistake #3 (and #4, and #5, and however many mistakes wearing a leather vest with scrubs adds up to).

At this point, waiting for my doctors to leave the room before I cried seemed to be a talent that I could teach at the master class level. It was a party trick I was using more and more often; more than any thirty-something woman should be willing to admit.

Who did this medical cowboy think he was?

Did he even talk to anyone else?

Or had he overridden their decision because he thought he knew what he was doing?

And why didn't I speak up?

I managed to dial my mother's number and weepily explained the situation.

"He just left, Mom. I didn't even get a chance to say anything. He's going to kill me."

"I'm on my way." She hung up before I could say anything or she could even ask me what the hell I was talking about.

My mother arrived in record time, just as the nurse practitioner for Douchey John Wayne came into the room. I enjoyed seeing her face. She was pleasant and kind, and didn't treat me like I was a moron. It also helped that she had never worn a leather vest (or any other vest, for that matter) over her scrubs. I barely gave her a chance to sit before I asked her what was going on.

"He doesn't know the new plan. You aren't getting another procedure here, I promise. He just hadn't talked to me before he came and saw you this morning."

Unbelievable. So, in he stormed, without so much as looking at my chart, and made a treatment plan for a patient he cared so little about that he hadn't even researched her disease. I rolled my eyes and verified one more time with her that he would never be touching me again. She confirmed and left the room before I could tell her what a jackhole I thought her boss was. Despite my trepidation about leaving to go to a new hospital, I was ecstatic that I would never have to deal with him or his dumb ass vest (that's the last time, I promise) again. He'd yelled at my family (true story) and talked down to me for the last time.

It was only two more days before the call came in. It was 8:00 p.m. on a Wednesday evening and I was just getting ready to take my nightly dose of Dilaudid and nod off until my sleep would be interrupted by the night staff. True to most of my experience thus far, it turned into a clusterfuck to include the wrong ambulance...

...wasn't aware you could have an INCORRECT ambulance, but you can...

...and I secretly hoped that I could get one more night with the staff I had come to know and care about.

(Okay, not so secretly, I wept like a baby when I found out I was leaving.)

But I just wanted, or *needed* would be more appropriate, one more night to prepare for the next leg of the race. Just one more night of familiarity before I was moved again and had to start over. What had begun as a sprint was quickly becoming a marathon, and I had not trained appropriately. Unfortunately, I was not given a choice, something that was quickly becoming a theme. Bright side? I had stopped crying every single day, so...silver lining. Perhaps my brain was finally trying to catch up to my emotions and I would finally learn how to cope with all things in my life being one big question mark.

Maybe.

CHAPTER FOURTEEN

The Teaching Hospital

January 2017 (Still)

Even though I was only being wheeled from the ambulance bay to my room, I could tell the hospital was massive. I knew from my previous and less emergent visits just how big the Vanderbilt campus was, but it was a different feeling, experiencing it from the interior. The sheer magnitude of the inside of the campus felt as if it was swallowing me as I was wheeled through the halls of the ER and up to my room on the eighth floor of what they called "the tower."

While I hadn't seen the outside of this particular building before, I pictured a castle that sat so high, clouds enveloped the outer walls, and I pictured the inside dank, cold, and uninviting. I was going to be the sickly princess with the three-month-old hair weave sitting in the tower and awaiting some form of rescue. I closed my eyes and tried to think of something other than the sick feeling in my stomach.

The panic I had felt when I was told I would be changing hospitals slowly crept its way back into my brain. I was brought back to the Dominican; an unfamiliar hospital, an unfamiliar bed, and unfamiliar staff. The feeling of not wanting Dan (and now my mother) to leave seemed to want to pour itself out of my tear ducts. I'd cried enough that day, so I stuffed them down, just far enough that I hoped they would not emerge until I was alone.

My room sat tucked in a corner at the end of a hallway. It was spacious but it had the look of a not-for-profit facility. The beige walls had certainly seen better days and the fancy amenities, new tile, and closet-sized bathroom left me longing to be back at my familiar hospital. What I would learn quickly is what it lacked in flash, it more than made up for with its clinical staff. None of that mattered that night, however. If I had to stay in a hospital, I wanted to go back to my other room, with my favorite nurse and my cable TV. I feared that, once again, I wouldn't sleep, although it appeared my pain medications had already been taken care of. At least something was going my way.

The ambulance staff finished their paperwork and left the room. I panned my surroundings and gazed out the window that took up the entire wall. I felt far away and alone. Even in the dark, I could literally feel the vastness of the campus and just how far it was from home. From what I could see, the grounds had the look of a SUNY college campus circa 1998; cold and spread-out. There were no trees, no landscaping, just the sight of red brick buildings expanding across asphalt. My old hospital was in my neighborhood and was convenient for visitors. There were trees. No one was going to visit me here. I gave my mother and Dan kisses and told them to go get some sleep.

"I'll be back first thing in the morning," my mom said. She hadn't spent one day away from the hospital since I had been admitted. Geography wasn't going to change that. Thank fucking goodness. She had no clue that her being there was the only tiny bit of glue holding me together.

The nurse came in shortly after to ask me all of the questions I had asked so many patients myself. It was clear he was new since his reaction to me telling him I drank a glass of wine every day was almost laughable.

"Seven days a week?" he said with a look of judgement on his face.

"Yes." *And you will too after a few more years of this job. Just saying. Don't judge me, asshat.*

He asked the remainder of his routine questions, put some sort of medication in my IV site (the fourth site so far), and left.

I flipped on the television and shut my eyes. As I listened to the sound of *Little People, Big World* or whatever happened to be on TLC at that moment, I drifted off to sleep. Sometime around 2:00 a.m., an unknown radiology tech came in for a chest x-ray. By the time I was discharged from the hospital, I would come to appreciate the familiarity of her face, even though I always saw it in the wee hours of the morning and usually after I had just drifted off to sleep after hours of being unable to deal with the pain and shut my mind off.

* * * * * * *

I'm going to say it again. I watch a lot of *Grey's Anatomy*. Remember? I watched so much I wondered if I could insert my own chest tube with no anesthesia or clue about what I was doing. Now, I understand that 95% of the things that happen on that show are false representations of the everyday operations of a hospital. For example, I know that if a doctor referred to an RN as "nurse" instead of using her name, that nurse would ignore the doctor purposely, or sarcastically reply "yes, physician."

I also know that the odds of the same person surviving a drowning, shooting, and plane crash are illogical. And I know when someone comes in to start my IV, that someone won't be a surgeon. They have better things to do with their time. And, they aren't good at it. All that being said, Shonda Rhimes got one thing right: at a teaching hospital, you are *never* alone. As a caveat to that, I was at a teaching hospital with a disease that most of the interns, residents, and attendings would only see once in their lifetime.

And I was their once in a lifetime.

Had it not been happening to me, I would have been in that room myself (meaning not as a patient, obviously), soaking up all the knowledge and relishing the idea of seeing something so rare. But it was me, which made it not interesting, not fun, and not at all enjoyable.

The first round of doctors came in at about 7:00 a.m. The head of the team was a short, grey-haired woman who worked hand in hand with my specialist. She was trailed by a group of interns who looked like they had just graduated from high school the previous year. One by one, they filtered into the room like a group of ducklings being led by their momma duck.

"It's nice to finally meet you. I've heard a lot about you from Dr. Young."

Apparently, my reputation preceded me. I wonder if she said that I was pleasant and quiet, or if she told the truth: I was sarcastic, a pain in the ass, and tended to swear more than the average sailor.

"How's your pain this morning?"

"Fine," I said. I didn't mean to sound curt in my response but I was genuinely surprised. She was the first physician who actually asked the question; perhaps it was just a formality but I still appreciated the gesture.

"Dr. Young told me you'd say that." She looked at me with the eyes of a mother who knew their child was lying to protect their feelings. The ducklings peered over each of her shoulders, soaking in all of the bedside manner they could. She walked over to the side of my bed and grabbed my hand. "How is it really?"

I wanted to leap out of the bed and hug her.

"It's pretty bad," I said. "I've had the chest tube in for about three weeks now and I'm pretty uncomfortable." It was still an understatement, so I added to it. "Actually, I'm very damn uncomfortable."

A well-placed "fucking" before the word uncomfortable would have been more on the nose; however, I wanted to ease her into to my potty-mouth demeanor.

She motioned to one of her ducklings, who immediately left the room, hopefully to write me an order. "Your pain control is important. Actually, for my purposes, it's the most important. So, I need you to be honest and I'll help you the best I can."

Once that was out of the way, she began to explain my treatment plan to me, something else that hadn't happened up until that point, and apparently something that would have quieted my brain down from overreacting, even just a tiny bit. Not only would I have a pulmonologist, but I would be seen by an interventional radiologist and a cardio-thoracic surgeon. The "dream team" would meet together and then attempt to come up with the best course of treatment with the highest likelihood of success. Unfortunately, there was no test or procedure they could perform to see if the first pleurodesis had been successful—and if it had been, if there was another reason my lung continued to leak. The hope was that the leak would heal itself, which would then allow my lung to stay inflated, which would then allow me to go home.

Seemed like a lot of things needed to go the right way when the last month had only seemed to prove the opposite.

She smiled as she told me the plan, and as much as I appreciated her optimism, I was not hopeful that it was how things would go down. I would be right in that thought, but not to any extent I could have imagined.

Round two was the interventional radiology team. The resident physician who led this team would quickly become my favorite part of the Vanderbilt experience. He was funny, witty, and compassionate. He walked into the room and introduced himself. Without so much as a hello, he said,

"Didn't I read about you in the paper?"

He really didn't miss a beat. Amidst all of the chaos of my ordeal, my story had made its way into the Nashville paper and several news outlets, a fact I hadn't really thought about since I didn't think people even read the paper anymore. Or watched the news. Or stayed informed.

"Yup. That was me," I said with a smile.

"Not to rub it in, but I went to the Dominican recently and it was amazing. Well, better than your trip, at least."

I laughed, something I had done so rarely lately that it made me feel good despite the pain it caused. He was sarcastic and clever, two traits rarely found in individuals with such high intellect. We were going to get along just fine, something that made me happy considering he was going to be rooting around in my lungs.

He discussed a lot of what the pulmonologist had, including that they would meet daily to discuss my case.

Funny, since the last surgeon didn't even have the wherewithal to call my specialist. Did I say wherewithal?

I meant compassion.

And intellect.

And general common fucking sense.

I mean, shit.

He also told me that they would do everything they could to avoid another surgery, but it looked like that was the avenue I was going to have to travel. He did a quick exam, casually asked me to take a deep breath as if that was an easy feat for me, and then told me he'd see me the following morning.

The final wave of visitors was my cardiothoracic team; a group of individuals that somehow made my condition feel like it was super important, which I suppose it was (and is).

I had two cardiothoracic surgeons, one a bit more socially inept than the other, but both were clearly brilliant, just like all of the other doctors that had crossed my threshold that day. I was learning quickly that all of the things I had heard about

Vanderbilt were true: a world-class hospital with some of the best physicians in the country. What they lacked in flair, they certainly made up for in the level of care delivered to their patients. Despite my meltdown the previous evening (and in the middle of the night, and a little bit early that morning), I was beginning to feel like things were getting back on track.

Amidst the intern questions and round three of a physical exam, my surgeon turned and looked at me almost as if he'd suddenly remembered that he'd left the oven on at home.

"The reason this treatment plan is so important is that if and when you need a lung transplant, it is as easy as possible. There are certain procedures that..."

He continued to talk but, in my mind, his voice became a whispered version of the teacher from Charlie Brown. There were only two words that were important to me.

Lung transplant.

They hung in the air like a stale odor. I was well aware that a lung transplant was a possibility, but hearing someone say it, out loud, to my face, about me—was extremely unnerving. It was nice to have the residents and interns present so they could ask all of the questions I didn't want to say out loud. I knew I was a long way away from a lung transplant, but the fact that it was even on the table made me want to throw up.

Eventually, I was alone in my room, left to ponder all of the new information that had been dumped on me. I had quickly gone from being in the care of an egotistic surgeon who felt I needed to know nothing about his plans to a baker's dozen of surgeons who felt like I needed to know every last detail about my care. While my peace of mind appreciated the plethora of knowledge that I was quickly gaining, the part of my brain that wanted to relax was longing for ignorance.

* * * * * * *

The first few days of my stay mirrored the previous hospital stay. No one seemed to know what the next steps were or why my lung did not want to do anything but cause problems. As I predicted, my visitors had become more sporadic, although they would sprinkle in throughout the weekend and break up my otherwise monotonous day-to-day existence. They brought jokes, more reading material, and one time, a batch of "all center-cut brownies" because they knew I hated the edges.

With nothing but time on my hands, and a month's worth of calling a hospital bed home, I decided I was educated enough to begin suggesting my own surgical procedures.

"What about exploratory surgery?" I asked one of the doctors on a morning I was feeling particularly intellectual and was choosing to ignore the fact that I had already been told this wouldn't work.

"Honestly, it would do more damage than good." He pity-smiled at me and said they would "figure something out."

And did they ever. Several times.

The first procedure on the list was called a blood patch, and it was probably the strangest procedure I'd had performed on me. Since the idiot surgeon at the previous hospital had done a half-assed version of a pleurodesis, there was hesitancy from the team at Vanderbilt to perform one again. There was a good chance if the first one had been done correctly (it hadn't), it would cause more damage to my already injured lung. In the interest of believing my previous surgeon wasn't completely incompetent, the team had come up with a plan that ended with a pleurodesis only as a last resort.

To perform a blood patch, one hundred gallons (or milliliters, if you do not appreciate the exaggeration) of your own blood is drained out of an IV site and then injected into your chest tube. Yes, it's as gross as it sounds and yes, I felt like there was a level of cannibalism to it. After the blood is in the pleural space, you literally roll around in bed like a beached whale for about an hour so that the blood coats the entire lung. The theory is that the blood will coagulate...

(I am vomiting a little in my mouth as I write this)

...and "fill" any holes that are causing the lung to remain Tom Brady-ed (see what I did there), thus decreasing the chance for infection and other medical complications.

I so badly wanted this creepy vampiric procedure to be my ticket home. I was already four days into my stay at Vanderbilt and I was more than ready to be surrounded by something familiar. That being said, optimism had not been my friend thus far, and I feared building a relationship now would not bode well for my psyche. I had a sneaking suspicion that this was not going to work.

I was right.

Two days later, it was on to step two, another experimental procedure which, in most situations, would have freaked me out. The past month had been many things, but it certainly didn't fall under the category of "most situations," so on the spectrum of things that bothered me, it was pretty low on the totem pole. I certainly had a better feeling about this procedure than I did about the vampire transfusion. The interventional radiology team would go into my lung and attempt to locate any hole that could be causing the leak. They would then insert valves into each hole that would cause air to enter but not exit. Kind of like the Hotel California of lung treatment.

The best part about the valve insertion is that I would get to go home once they were placed, which, up until that point, had seemed like it would never happen. In six weeks, the valves would be removed and my lungs would finally be healed. I couldn't wait. One month in and I was going to be able to close this chapter of my life and never look back. This was going to work.

Spoiler alert: it didn't.

It wasn't long before the valves were in, my hose of a chest tube was replaced with a smaller version, and I was being wheeled out of the hospital and on my way home. It had been twenty-four days, three chest tubes, six IV sites, three procedures, and more Dilaudid than a junkie could handle, but none of that was important anymore. I was going home. I'm glad I didn't know all of the pain I would still have to go through, or how many more days I would spend in the hospital, because, if I had, the catharsis of that moment would have been ruined. And that moment, that feeling, is one of the few I cherish from the entire year.

CHAPTER FIFTEEN

The Cost of Doing Illness

There's no real good way to segue into this but, considering I just talked about how much time I spent in a hospital, this is as good a spot as any to throw this in. I feel as if I should warn you, there is a good chance this next part comes off trite and ungrateful.

Not in a fun way.

Not in a "oh, she's selfish but still witty" kind of way.

In a way that has the potential to make me seem like there was only a certain amount of money I was willing to spend to keep myself alive. Because we all know that can't possibly be true, right? I mean, considering how many times I've referenced my fear of dying, it would be insane for me to put a price cap on my health.

But, I'm gonna.

Honestly, I'm not sure there isn't anything I wouldn't do to stay alive if given the option. That being said, just because I *would* pay it doesn't mean I should.

All of those things aside, there was one giant hurdle: I could not figure out why I was unable to write these thoughts down without the words seeming meaningless. My fear was I would write all of this down and someone would wonder what the point was. And nothing is worse than words for the sake of filling space. After sitting on it for a bit, I realized that I truly had to step back on this one; that the things I wanted to talk about needed to be said, but not from a place of anger. And I stay angry about this next topic, so it proved a difficult task to complete.

Not to mention, it's boring as fuck.

And, if I'm being honest? I was also kind of afraid it would negatively affect my job; insulting your company's policies doesn't necessarily bode well for promotions and accolades. I worked hard for my career and have come a long way from the girl who took a random job just because it meant she didn't have to drive on the interstate.

But fuck it. I haven't let my fear of looking like an asshole stop me so far, so let's get into it.

This chapter won't be long. And it likely won't be laced with as many of the sarcastic and witty quips you have come to expect and love from yours truly. But the length of the chapter is not directly related to the significance of the subject matter. It's just much more succinct; likely because that is how I have to store it in my brain so I don't become overwhelmed. And bitter.

I first decided that I wanted to include this chapter when I got a bill in the mail that was, among others, unanticipated. Now, I've had unexpected bills before—you don't spend months in and out of a hospital without accruing some sort of running tab that is so high you have to borrow against your 401K to pay it. But once the dust settles from that experience, it was my belief that the cost of being chronically ill would be no different than that cost of being well.

Not. True.

Not in the least.

Once you have that diagnosis, be it cancer, or LAM, or some other disease you didn't ask for but are unlucky enough to have, you will literally pay for that diagnosis until the day you die. And maybe even after (which is just one more reason death sounds absolutely awful). Given that medical bills are not unique to my condition, I want to talk about the true cost of being sick. Not the emotional cost, or physical limitations, but the actual monetary burden of spending the remainder of your life chronically ill.

First things first. Insurance is bullshit. I had an inkling that this was true shortly after I began working in the medical field, but the concept was really driven home after I began my work in insurance denials. I spent my days writing letters to insurance companies to prove to them a procedure was medically necessary, even though the doctor believed it to be. Even after authorizations, letters of medical necessity, and the blood of a virgin, they may or may not decide to pay it. Yes. That's a thing. Insurance companies can be like, "Nah, I'm all set," and refuse to pay a claim. As infuriating as that is, it's the truth.

And the things they refuse to pay for are unreal. It would make you sick.

What I didn't ever expect was to be the person on the other side of the letter. The patient who could not for the life of me figure out how to get my bills covered, even though it was literally what I did for a living. (I don't know how any layperson figures shit like this out; I guess they just pay the bill whether they are contractually obligated to or not.)

I've jumped through every hoop, gone up the chain until I was so high I developed vertigo, I've begged, I've pleaded, I've appealed the case until I have nothing else to say. And still, if I paid all of my medical bills (which I don't—and I couldn't care less that I owe that money) that weren't covered for whatever reason, I'd be in a financial hole so deep I don't know how I'd dig myself out.

But, out of sight out of mind.

The bills come and they go directly into the shredder.

And if someone has the nerve to say something to me in person, I pretend I'm going to "get right on that."

I'm not.

This is the thing. Insurance is great when you're healthy—you pull out your Andrew Jackson, pay your copay at a well visit, and are none the wiser. Maybe you don't get that extra Starbucks coffee that week, but you are no worse off financially, just slightly less caffeinated. Maybe you have to pay out of pocket for a test here and there—that's what savings is for—but in your normal everyday life, once you pay your monthly premium, you are covered.

(Whew. This is really boring, I know. Just stick with me).

Sadly, this is not how it works with chronic illness. At least I assume I am not alone in this boat. Let me start by breaking down the cost (in very rudimentary terms). For the purposes of sticking with what I know, I am going to talk about LAM specifically.

First, let's talk about the number of clinics that treat LAM in the United States. There are currently thirty-one total LAM clinics, meaning places that have actually heard of my disease and treated LAM patients in the past. Thirty. One. In the entire country. Now, as you know at this point, I don't believe in God or fate, so let's just say that by luck, I ended up in a city where one of these LAM clinics was located. I have never had to travel for my treatment or get misdiagnosed by a doctor simply because the disease is so rare they have never seen it before.

My insurance does NOT pay for this specialist.

In fact, they *refuse* to pay for any visit because the facility where my doctor practices is considered out of network because it is not the preferred hospital of my insurance.

"You can see any lung specialist," they will tell you.

Forget the rarity of your disease and that someone who has made LAM their life's work is in the same town as you. Just go to our doctor. Because we say so.

"Get your testing one place and go to your doctor in another."

Yes, because historically, that has always gone off without a hitch. You've never lost my labs, done the wrong test, or refused to speak to my doctor at all.

"This is some of the best insurance coverages you will ever have."

Unless you're sick.

And it's all pretty easy for them to say. The people making these decisions have either never had to endure the burden of a life-altering diagnosis, or they make so much money, paying hundreds of dollars for a doctor's visit doesn't affect them in the least.

Sadly, I do not have that luxury. Here is the breakdown of what I pay if nothing at all goes wrong:

Each out-of-pocket visit costs me roughly $1,000, give or take. Depending on the results of my lung function testing and if my breathing has deteriorated, I see my specialist anywhere between two to six times per year. If we average that, I go to the doctor four times per year. That's $4,000 per year for those of you too lazy to do the math.

(Disclaimer: I am not going into detail about the cost of prescriptions because I have been very lucky in that regard, and my prescriptions are [mostly] covered by my insurance. That being said, I do want to acknowledge that the rarer the disease, the less likely the medication to treat it comes in a generic form and/or is covered by insurance. And this can cripple people financially and should not be ignored. I just cannot speak on it personally...as of today.)

This next bill was the hardest pill to swallow (bad choice of words, I know, given the above, but I can't resist a pun). I sat in my office opening the piles of mail I'd allowed to stack up, and discovered that although I thought my oxygen was being paid for, it was not.

Not only did I get to be a forty-something woman (let's be clear though, I look thirty-something on my best days) who was going to be on oxygen for the rest of my life, but I was also going to have to pay for that oxygen. My knowledge of science is elementary, but I am 99% sure that humans require oxygen. To live.

Following the myriad of surgeries performed on my lung, I became someone who had to think about oxygen, and who my supplier would be. Again, I assumed that if the company that provided my oxygen was "in network," that would mean my oxygen was paid for.

Any guesses on whether or not that is the case?

It's not.

I am entirely convinced that the phrase "in network" is something made up that is just supposed to make people feel better and it actually means jack shit when it comes to what the insurance actually pays for.

I pay for my oxygen out of pocket. Every month. Even though, as we learned in third grade science class, oxygen is a requirement for human survival. And I can hear some people now. The reason I didn't want to say any of this.

"But you can't put a price on your health."

The fuck I can't.

Maybe not for surgery or extreme life-saving measures, but for my oxygen? The price for that should be free.

I've only used the next phrase twice in this entire book, so I feel I am due for at least one more.

It's not fair. Like seriously, not fair.

And I've tried to fight it. I've gone up each and every ladder until I was standing on the top rung and reaching for something to steady myself. The request makes it so far and then I inevitably end up with the same answer I heard from the person before: there is nothing we can do.

In fact, maybe we should be the ones getting paid. For the inconvenience of it all.

Yes, you heard me. Pay the sick. Like mother-fucking Robin Hood.

Insurance companies should take the billions of dollars

they earn each year, and offer financial compensation to those of us who have what can only be described as daily crippling anxiety because we were dealt a shitty fucking hand. And before you say, "but that would affect them financially," let me assure you, that is not even the least bit true. And if it is, so what? They can take the hit. I want financial compensation for the physical and mental toll having LAM has had on me.

Since I'm a numbers person, let's look at some for the sake of the argument.

My particular insurance provider, United Healthcare, made $270 billion in 2020. Yes. BILLION.

The CEO alone made a cold $17.87 million in total compensation the same year.

BlueCross BlueShield took a "financial hit" in 2020 and still made just over $30 billion.

Cigna? A measly $8.5 billion.

It clearly is not about the money for them, but it is for me. If they covered just my healthcare, that would equate to three mortgages per year. Or ten car payments. Or all of my utility bills, plus a little left over.

But, at the very least?

Pay for my oxygen, you trolls.

CHAPTER SIXTEEN

The Homecoming
January and February 2017

My 1,600 square foot cottage-style house felt like a palace.

Everything that had happened over the past month suddenly seemed like it was a lifetime ago. The nightmare was quickly forgotten as I walked through the front door and scanned the contents of my home. I was going to get to sleep in my own bed (actually, I would be on the couch, but...semantics), I was going to get to cuddle my puppy, I was going to take an actual shower instead of a whore's bath out of a basin, and most importantly, I was going to eat something other than hospital food or three bites of broccoli cheddar soup from Panera or Au Bon Pain.

The only thing that could have made my homecoming just a bit sweeter was if I had been able to come home sans any chest tube at all. That being said, while it was painful, if it meant that I got to recover in my own surroundings, I was good with it.

Dan took my arm and led me towards the couch. "Welcome home, baby."

The three words hit me like I had just taken a hit off a

bong. I could feel the tension, which had probably been present since that morning in the Dominican, leave my shoulders

I didn't know what else to say, so I just said, "Thank you."

I wanted to cry but I had done enough of that, despite the fact that they would be happy tears this time. Instead, I said nothing else and I let him guide me to the couch that had already been converted to a bed, pending my arrival. Despite the fact that I had been in a bed for the past month, I couldn't wait to lie down in a familiar place and close my eyes, knowing I wouldn't be woken up to the sound of interns or portable chest x-rays.

My mother and Dan's parents arrived shortly after to help get us settled into to our new routine. I wonder now if that was more for Dan's sake than mine.

Certainly, it was. And rightly so.

He'd managed to stay pretty put together through all of this, despite his anxiety that had most definitely reached a new level of intensity. Having some emotional support couldn't hurt things. On top of that (and I am not saying anything he wouldn't say himself), there was no fucking way he could drain bloody fluid out of my chest tube.

Actually, while we're talking about it, neither could my mother. Although she'd be more likely to try than Dan, I could just picture her turning her head the other way while trying to unscrew the mechanism, all while attempting not to throw up in her mouth.

Welcome to the shit show.

I lay down on the couch and immediately felt more exhausted than I had all day. I felt a slight fever coming on, something I had experienced since my pre-teen years, but I didn't care. I had a dog curled up at my feet and the sounds of conversing family had replaced the sound of beeping medical equipment and ornery patients. I felt my eyelids closing as my mother asked if I was hungry. I mumbled something I hoped was at least mildly coherent and drifted off to sleep.

* * * * * * *

I have a difficult time pulling positives from any negative experience, but this one especially. Thankfully, in situations like these, people like to present you with their own silver linings in order to ease the pain of reality.

At least you're alive. (Okay, that one is probably true.)

At least you weren't in Mexico. (Whatever that means.)

At least you're home now. (Again, that one is true.)

Being off of work for a while? It's like a mini-vacation. (Not so much.)

You can catch up on TV. (Obviously.)

It could be worse. (Well...)

Despite the fact that I was home and was no longer forced to eat shit hospital food while I stared out a window at a parking lot, this was NOT a mini-vacation, and the novelty of just being anywhere but the hospital had very quickly worn off. The chest tube, albeit smaller than the last, still created unnecessary discomfort and to top it all off, the isolation was clearly getting to me.

I couldn't drive, couldn't leave my house, still couldn't take a shit (that's another issue altogether), and still couldn't shower alone. While it was true I was no longer in the hospital, it was a far cry from a vacation and (I can't believe I'm about to say this next part) there are only so many times you can rewatch *Friends*.

I tried, on several occasions, to convince my mother that she could go home and visit my sister who had just given birth to her first grandchild that November. It wasn't that I didn't want her with me, but every time she did something nice, I felt a twinge of guilt for being her "problem child," especially since I was taking time away from her enjoying being a grandmother. I was thirty-four and being nursed back to health by my mother; her life had been consumed with seeing my face, putting up with my tantrums, and knitting scarves to pass the endless hours.

Of course, she insisted on staying and despite my culpability, I was glad she did not take me up on my offer. I wasn't ready to be alone yet. And there was a good chance I hadn't even begun to process what exactly had transpired over the last month. It was not a stretch to say that I could have died in that filthy hospital while Dan tried to get me on a plane back home.

I had a feeling that last thought was not lost on my mother either.

"I know you feel guilty, but I'm where I want to be," she would say every few days. Was it true? I'm not sure.

Was she saying it to convince me, as well as herself? Probably.

The days seemed to be endless, one almost seamlessly blurring into the next. I spent nearly twenty-four hours a day on the couch, watching horrid daytime TV and napping on and off. My mother ran errands, attempted to get me to eat, and bought jug after jug of apple juice in an effort to help me get things "moving." Dan was finally able to go back to work, and I was happy to see him back in some sort of routine. At least he could spend a few hours a day not reminded that he was stuck with an invalid for a girlfriend.

Sometimes I cried, sometimes I talked, and sometimes I threw my phone across the room so that everyone knew I was mad enough to break my own possessions.

I rarely smiled, and I almost never laughed.

"I'm good, I swear," I would say to anyone who asked; my entire demeanor was becoming very reminiscent of my attitude when I had first been diagnosed. It was amazing how quickly I was able to slip back into the melancholy.

Somewhere during my stint at three different hospitals, I had convinced myself that once I was out of the hospital, the old me would make an appearance, even intermittently. And yet, I found myself turning into a quiet, depressed introvert; three words that I never would have used to describe myself.

I knew that I was pushing my friends away and building a wall around myself but, despite my knowledge that was the case, I couldn't stop myself. And Dan. My sweet man-friend who had been nothing but kind and present through my whole ordeal had become my punching bag. Sometimes, okay most times, I am surprised he stayed, although I imagine there was a part of him that thought it would look bad if he left in the midst of everything. But I wouldn't have blamed him. I still wouldn't.

No one would.

* * * * * * *

Somewhere in the midst of all of my negativity, my sister and my mother planned a visit from the only person who had the power to change my mood—my nephew. He was the perfect specimen of adorableness and I was happy that she didn't have an ugly baby, because I certainly didn't have the energy to fake my way through calling him "cute" if he wasn't. Luckily, her and her husband's genes had transferred flawlessly to my nephew. He was like a breath of fresh air (or just a regular deep breath in my case).

I had a brief moment of panic, wondering if seeing my mother with her grandchild, and knowing I could not give that happiness to her, would trigger old feelings of inadequacy; however, the love I immediately had for him overrode any of that. The thought was fleeting and did not stay long enough to ruin a single moment of my time with him.

In addition to my nephew, my sister's laugh was a welcome addition to my otherwise morose attitude. If you know her, you know her laugh is...distinct. Infectious. Loud. It's almost impossible not to at least smile when the sound exits her mouth. I missed it. And her. While we hadn't always seen eye-to-eye, as adults we had become true friends, just like I had always hoped.

"It's so good to see you," she said one night when we were the only two awake.

"You too," I replied. "I'm so sorry I—"

She stopped me before even knowing what I was going to apologize for. "I love you." The words came out in a way that made me feel like she loved me more in that moment than she ever had before.

"I love you too," I said.

The two days they spent at the house seemed to fly by, as most happy moments do. As mine seemed to be more fleeting as of late, this one went particularly fast. I said my goodbyes, kissed my beautiful nephew, and found my place back on the sofa that now had an imprint of my ass permanently stamped into the fabric.

What now?

I had the removal of my chest tube to look forward to, followed by the removal of my valves, and then...

With the arrival of my nephew now in my rear view, I feared that I would quickly fall back into my depression. The only "good news" I had scheduled was medical, and I was exhausted from thinking about nothing but my lung, and the oxygen I'd been on since discharge, and the chest tube that leaked fluid all over everything I owned.

Dan was back at work and, shortly after my sister left, my mother followed. Despite the guilt I had felt for the duration of her visit, I wanted to ask her to stay; to tell her I couldn't do this without her; to whine like I did as a four-year-old who wanted to be carried instead of walking across the hot sand (something I allegedly used to do regularly). But I kept my mouth shut. I promised her I would be fine and told her she'd put off her life long enough.

The next month was a mix of Netflix binges, first nap, random visitors, second nap, and puppy cuddles. Despite thinking the days would drag by, before I knew it, my mother was back to take me for my final surgery.

I could see the end in sight. The valves would get removed, the lung would finally have healed itself, and I could get back to bitching about my shitty commute and boring life. I could start eating normal food and shitting on a regular basis and wearing a bra. I would get to see my friends because I wanted to, not because they had to come to me to make sure I wasn't on the brink of a nervous breakdown (I was). If I needed something at the store, I could get in my car and get it. Not make Dan go back out after a long day of work because I finally had a craving for something.

I was finally going to be able to say that this chapter of my life was finished...

...not.

* * * * * * *

Six weeks later, I was back at the hospital. Not for a medical emergency this time, it was finally time to have the valves removed and (hopefully) be able to start healing. This was it. While I was not a fan of being put under again, the end result was going to make all the rest of it okay. Even the surgeons seemed optimistic, a feeling that had not been the norm when discussing whether or not the procedure I was having done on any particular day was going to work.

Dan was there with me, of course, and sat next to me while we waited to go back.

"This is it," he said. And he meant it. That was the first time he'd sounded sure of something in such a long time, and the words felt like I was being wrapped in a warm blanket.

"I fucking hope so," I replied. Hope was all I had since I wasn't even close to believing this was all going to work. I could not imagine a scenario where things would de-escalate.

He held my hand while the nurses scurried in and out of the room, hooking up my IV, taking vitals, and making sure I was comfortable. My friend Angie, always the fixer, even sent one of her close friends who was a nurse at Vanderbilt down to check on me and make sure they were "treating me well." I did a mental exhale and closed my eyes.

Everything was going to be okay.

I awoke from surgery number five to the face of my favorite interventional radiologist (yes, I had a favorite). In his hand, he held the valves that had taken up temporary residence in my lungs for the past six weeks. In my anesthesia-laden state, there is a good chance I had told him I loved him, which was not entirely untrue. He had accomplished what is nearly impossible at a teaching hospital: making me feel like I was his only patient despite what I can only imagine is a nearly impossible workload.

Originally, the plan had been to keep me overnight for observation just in case; something that made sense given the events of the last few months.

"But the surgery went really well," the doctor said, "and I imagine you're over being in a hospital bed."

He had no idea.

"Ummm, I'm all set. I'd like to get the hell out of here. No offense."

"And don't take this the wrong way," he said with a comforting smile, "but I'd really like to not see you for a while."

He handed me a sealed jar that contained the valves that he said I could keep to remember him by, and disappeared behind the curtain surrounding my bed. I'd miss him, but I was certainly looking forward to not seeing his face for a bit.

"Let's get out of here." Dan pushed my wheelchair out of the main doors and we waited for the car to pull to the curb.

As we drove home, I felt a sense of calm wash over me. All of the panic, all of the anxiety, all of the depression suddenly melted away and was replaced with a new emotion that had been a foreign concept the last few months: hope. The last time I had felt this at ease was the first night we spent in the Dominican; when the white sheets and the ocean breeze allowed my brain to focus solely on the moment and how good it felt.

I was finally done and the only remnants of my ordeal would be my souvenir valves and the oxygen I'd have to wear until I could build up my lung capacity. When we finally got back to the house, my mother was waiting for us. She had returned, despite my pleading for her to stay on her Florida vacation; one of the very few things she actually did for herself.

"They are just taking the valves out. It is an outpatient procedure and I'll be fine."

But, as I expected, she came anyway. "You don't get to tell me what to do."

True. I could pretend otherwise, but one thing about my mother had been true for my entire life. Once her mind was made up, it would take an act of God (or the atheist equivalent) to change her mind. At least during the start of this visit, I felt like I could enjoy her company instead of feeling like a thirty-something-year-old invalid.

Dan's family was also in town and provided a welcome change of scenery. I was finally able to move around on my own, albeit slow as hell, since I was no longer on oxygen 24/7. Other than not being cleared to drive, I felt more like myself than I had in months. Dan's stepmother comforted me with Italian food, his dad with humor, and my mom brought the carbohydrates and sarcasm. Other than the occasional checking of my oxygen, we didn't even talk about my lungs, or about how harrowing the last few months had truly been.

It was glorious.

But I got too comfortable. I should have known better.

I ran up the stairs when I should have run out the front door.

And I don't mean this in a brooding or self-pity kind of way. I mean it in a medically-I-should-have-known-better-because-I'm-a-nurse kind of way.

CHAPTER SEVENTEEN

The Return
March, 2017

Things were so good. So. Fucking. Good.

I had my dog, my Dan, my mom, and zero foreign objects in my body. It had only been twenty-four hours since I was last in the hospital, but it may as well have been a month. I felt so far removed from the whole ordeal that I could finally begin to think about my life moving forward. It would only be another few weeks before I could get back to work and feel like I was living my real life and not some Lifetime movie.

The next part happened so quickly that I barely had time to process it.

The second night after I had the valves removed, I was sitting on the couch when, after a deep breath, I felt odd. Different. No pain, just foggy, almost like that very first day back in December of 2014. I knew then. My lung had collapsed. I coughed several times, which piqued the interest of my caretakers.

"You okay?" Dan was immediately at my side with an O2 sensor outstretched.

"I'm fine," I lied. "It was just a cough. My O2 is going to be low; I haven't had my oxygen on."

I had to make sure that I calmly addressed what I knew

was coming next; a low oxygen number with Dan and my mom concerned that the worst had happened (which it had). If they thought I expected it for a different reason, maybe they would think everything was fine. Apparently, my fake confidence had allowed them to believe me.

"Okay," he said as he pulled the sensor off my finger. "Put your oxygen on, okay?" As he had so many times before, he kissed my forehead and, as I had so many times in recent history, I held back tears.

"We know it's annoying," my mom chimed in. "But we need to make sure we do all we can to keep you out of the hospital again."

Well. It's a bit late for that.

Dan and I had our issues, and my mom and I fought sometimes; but one thing we didn't do was lie to each other, at least not about the important stuff. Do I lie about my feelings to protect others? To downplay a specific situation? Sometimes. But, when it comes down to important things, my health being one of them, I pride myself on being 100% honest. And as far as my mom was concerned, I had been scared to lie to her since I was young. Hell, I still was.

The lie was going to happen today, however. Partly because I knew the collapse was small at the current moment—and with oxygen, I was almost positive I could make it through the night before having to let someone know—and partly because I also wanted to lie to myself. To relish in the positivity I had only had the pleasure of experiencing for twenty-four hours.

The plan was simple: get through the night and then pretend it had happened early the next morning so that I could enjoy one more night of normalcy.

And just maybe, I would get to the hospital, have a chest x-ray, and be proven a paranoid hypochondriac. Then Dan and Peg could laugh at my gross overreaction and go back to scolding me for trying to do too much too fast.

The following morning, I told my mother I felt "strange"

and that the feeling had just happened all of a sudden. I didn't elaborate or compare my symptoms, so I am not sure if my mother or Dan believed the story I had concocted about waking up and just "feeling weird." If they didn't, neither of them mentioned it. Dan went off to work and my mother loaded me into the car and made the familiar drive to Vanderbilt. She had been there so often that she was able to do it without GPS assistance, which was a huge deal.

"How are you feeling?" she asked when we were about halfway to the hospital.

"I don't think it's anything." The lies kept coming. Apparently, I had just needed to rip the off the Band-Aid. "Probably just residual pain from the valve procedure."

She smiled and turned back towards the road. She thought I was full of shit. Damn, she was good.

We valeted the car and trekked down the hall (yes, another long hallway for people with compromised lungs) to the outpatient radiology department. I pretended I wasn't all too familiar with the chest x-ray process and let the technicians give me the rundown without telling them they could save their spiel for someone who gave a shit.

Because I really didn't. But I kept my mouth shut, took my bra off in front of another stranger, and allowed the radiation to flow through my body.

Per my doctor's instructions (Dan had texted her to let her know we were on our way), my mother and I sat in the waiting room waiting for her to read the results and give me the okay to go home. I suddenly felt extremely foolish. Here I was, barely one day postop, panicking and thinking my lung had collapsed. Seriously, it was probably just whatever remaining trauma response I had popping up to say hello.

So, I "felt odd."

So, I'd coughed.

So, what?

Some of the best physicians in the country told me that the

odds of my lung collapsing again in the next few months were less than 1%, and yet I had convinced myself that they were wrong and I was right.

Well. I was right.

Amidst a game of Words with Friends or some other mindless app, my phone rang. I saw Dr. Young's all too familiar number appear on my screen.

That was sweet of the doctor to call instead of text, I thought as I walked around the corner to take the call.

"I'm so sorry."

My inner monologue was screaming the word "fuck" over and over again. I stayed silent.

She didn't have to say anything after that, but she did. My fear only allowed me to listen to bits and pieces of her instructions; thankfully I'd had the forethought to put the phone on speaker.

"Another pneumothorax...admitted for another pleurodesis...chest tube placement..." At the end of the conversation (but not really, because I just sat silent on the other end of the line and contributed nothing more than awkwardness), she instructed me where to go and I hung up the phone, completely defeated.

My mother looked up from her phone as I turned the corner.

"Fuck." This time I said it out loud. The tears started once again and I wondered if I was setting some sort of world record.

"I am so sorry." She gave me a hug, but instead of hugging her back, I just let my arms hang limp at my sides like two spaghetti noodles.

I didn't have it in me to do this again.

Literally. There was no way.

I. Was. Exhausted.

I already knew that the surgery to correct Dr. Rhinestone Cowboy's original fuckup would be extremely more painful than the first. Not only that, but because they had to do a more vigorous procedure, it was essentially the same as using talc. So, in the very basic sense, they were going to cement my lung to my chest wall to keep it from collapsing again (or, at least decrease the chances by 75-ish%). Which was great until I had to get a lung transplant and I bled out on the table because they were trying to chisel an organ out of my chest.

Shit. My mind had clearly started to race and I was too slow to stop it. The words of my thoracic surgeon played on repeat in my head.

This will make a transplant more difficult.

There will be a higher risk of bleeding.

You'll have to find a surgeon who is comfortable doing a more intricate procedure.

Write your will.

Say goodbye.

Granted, I'd been told that my odds of requiring a transplant were slim to none, but all of the past events had proven that "the odds" and I didn't really get along. As I sat planning my funeral and wondering who I could trust to delete my Facebook page search history, my mother was on the phone filling someone in, likely Dan or my sister.

My mind was reeling as I sat in the holding tank, waiting for an available room. I made friends with an extremely eccentric amputee who wanted to talk about anything and everything while we both waited to be admitted. I silently hoped that our rooms were nowhere in the vicinity of each other. Normally, small talk didn't bother me, but today was different. I did my best to appear interested and, just when I thought I was going to have to yell "Just shut the hell up" to a woman who was doing nothing but being kind, I was told I had a room.

"How are we feeling today?" asked the kind man who was transporting me to my room.

He was either going to get sarcasm or a lie. I choose the latter.

"I'm good. Really good. I'm doing fine."

I know it sounded put on, but my brain was far too preoccupied to concentrate on my acting ability.

Unlike my last visit, my room was not at the end of the hall but right outside the nurse's station. It was busy and loud and the room was one-third the size of my previous room. Being admitted during the day was also vastly different from my overnight admission. As soon as I was in the room and on the bed, there were three staff members crammed into the closet-sized space with me, asking me all the questions and doing their assessments.

I knew the drill. Vital signs. Oxygen. A quick judgmental look when I tell them how much I drink. And then would come the worst of it.

Another chest tube.

Even though I had spent the better part of the new year with a hose lodged inside my pleural space, it did not prepare me for the feeling again. Additionally, despite all of my previous medical ordeals, I had never been awake when they inserted one of the larger chest tubes and I was not looking forward to being conscious while they fed a tub into the hole they had cut into my body.

The procedure was inevitable. And just like I thought it would, it sucked. Hard.

On a very small positive note, dissimilar to most of my other experiences, my pain mediation had been taken care of before my feet had even hit the floor. Even better, the nurse who came to provide me with my much-needed relief was my favorite nurse from the previous admission. Her name was Adele and while, as I may have mentioned once or twice, I don't believe in signs, as an avid music lover and a singer, a nurse with the name of one of the most talented vocalists out there couldn't have been a fluke.

She smiled as she walked towards my bed. "I was hoping I was wrong, but I knew it was you." She squeezed my hand.

"I'd ask how you were doing but…"

Before I could even ask, she was injecting the coveted Dilaudid into my arm.

"I'm happy it's you," I told her. Luckily, I got the words out before the medicine had truly hit me and, instead of giving her a compliment, started singing "Water Under the Bridge" to her in a slurred and off-key voice.

"I'm here all night. I've got you."

She left the room with one more smile and I relished the idea that I would get some drug-induced rest.

At some point during my half-asleep state, I was greeted by the interventional radiologist I'd sworn I wouldn't see again and a new member of my ever-growing medical team.

I made a comment about how much I'd missed him and he laughed even though the joke was only funny on a "dad joke" level at best. We discussed the plan for tomorrow's surgery (the sixth for those of you keeping track) and as we talked, I recalled the post-surgical pain that was so crippling I had been rendered speechless. There was no way I was going to go through that again without speaking up.

"So, this is going to hurt, right?"

"Yes," the new doctor replied.

"And you'll give me meds. Lots of them?" I knew I sounded like the textbook "drug seeker" I had learned so much about during my nursing career, but I didn't care.

New doctor paused, looked at me, and uttered the most beautiful four-word phrase I'd ever heard in my entire life.

"You bet your ass."

He really was the best.

Despite my chest tube, and my IV tube, and the lack of cable, I actually slept well that night. Sadly, it was as if I had become immune to the idea of a radical surgery and the role it would consistently play in my life.

Everything the following day moved quickly. My surgery was scheduled for 7:00 a.m. the following morning and no one was dragging their feet this time. I was rolled out of my room at 6:00 a.m. on the dot and taken to preoperative suite to meet my anesthesiologist and get prepped for the procedure. I had not had a chance to talk to Dan or my mother before I was taken down, but someone did because right before I left my room I got a text that they were already in the waiting room.

Loyal as hell, those two. And worried. Too worried to stay at home where they would be forty minutes out if something went wrong.

Thankfully, nothing did. I left the operating room with three chest tubes (yes, three whole chest tubes) and one catheter that I apparently kept forgetting I had because I asked someone every five minutes if I had a catheter in and if I was okay to "go ahead and pee."

I waved hello to Dan and my mom when I got back to the room and was transferred back to my bed. It was odd, but I was not feeling the pain I thought I would after such an extensive and traumatic surgery. Apparently, that was because there is a numbing agent that can be injected into your body cavity and, though I have not been paid to endorse this medication, I highly recommend it. Frankly, this medication is given to anyone who has the misfortune of having a procedure that involves "agitating the pleural space."

Now, of course I didn't feel great. Who would? But the pain was minimal and not anything that I expected post a four-hour scraping of my insides. I also didn't have to move to go to the bathroom, something that proved extremely useful in my drug-induced stupor.

Unfortunately, all of these feelings would be short-lived. The pain was coming, and I was NOT prepared.

On day three, I was reminded why the month-long constipation that comes with regular opiate use was worth it. The numbing medication had worn off and I was left with both pain and a new and odd feeling. Any time I moved, it felt like I was drowning. Literally. I may as well have been gasping for air and inhaling water instead.

As long as I lay in my bed, I could bear the pain, but the minute I got up, it was as if my head was being held underwater and the pain level increased exponentially. The idea of taking a deep breath made me sick to my stomach. I no longer had a catheter and the bathroom that was only three steps away from my bed may as well have been on the other side of the hospital.

That evening, I was "encouraged" to begin ambulating and attempted my first laps around the unit.

"Take your time, I'll be right here." My mother, steadfast as ever, looked up from her chair to make sure I knew all I had to do was say the word and she'd be with me. Thirty-something years old and yet, I needed her just as much as I did when I was a kid.

"Thank you."

I began the slow walk around the unit and, in that moment, I would have rather died as I stood there than take another single step. The commute was slow, painful, and almost futile, since it felt in that moment like my lungs would never heal from all of the suffering they had been through.

My walking schedule was the same as an older gentleman who reminded me of my grandfather and smiled every time he passed. It was a nice distraction from the nursing assistant who wanted to talk about why I didn't look like my mother and when I told her it was because I was adopted, responded with, "Well, I'm sure she loves you anyway."

Every once in a while, he would give me a thumbs-up and say something like "Good job, kiddo." I'd always smile back though I was never able to say anything back to him. If only I could have told him how much he motivated me those first few days.

I had only made it one lap around the floor before I refused to walk anymore and requested I get put back to bed. While I know now that I sounded like a whiny bitch and the worst kind of patient, at that moment, there wasn't anything anyone could say to me that would have convinced me to walk one more step.

Good thing I would be awakened at 6:00 a.m. by a doctor who believed that the best way to motivate a patient was the sheer power of jack-assery. He strolled into the room with his entourage and, before I could even wipe the sleep out of my eyes, began what would be a brief (and curt) conversation.

"You have blood in your pleural space."

His lack of segue should have been my first clue. But since my eyes still had crusted bits in the corners, I cannot be blamed for believing that sarcasm would be the proper response to a doctor who couldn't even introduce himself.

"Well, that's good news," I said. Sarcastically. Actually, I said it *extremely* sarcastically as to not create confusion.

This doctor was not fluent in sarcasm. In fact, he had never even visited sarcasm and I doubt he had ever even told a knock-knock joke.

"No. It's not."

Okay. Noted. I opened my mouth to speak, but before I could explain myself, he continued with his guilt trip.

"And I heard you won't even walk. Do you want all of the doctors who worked so hard to have done it for nothing? Because that's what you're doing. You're making this all worthless."

His minions stood behind him in silence, as if this was his status quo.

Pussies.

Who did he think he was?

Even as I asked the question to myself, I didn't care. It could have been God Himself, and he would have had no reason to speak to me that way. If someone told me this story as a nurse, I would have probably said they were full of shit, or at least exaggerating, but I swear that this is exactly how it went down. I'd had my fair share of dealing with douchey doctors

173

and their weird attitudes, but this was the first time I wanted to punch one directly in the face.

I managed to maintain composure while he spouted condescending nonsense for several more minutes. He left the room and, once again, as I had countless times in the past few months, I immediately burst into tears. My ability to hold in a meltdown at least meant he wouldn't get to relish in the glee he surely would have experienced knowing he made me cry.

I sent a quick text to my mom letting her know she needed to add one more to her list of people that needed to wind up missing and then I immediately called my nurse into the room. Before she could even get to my bedside, I was making sure she knew where I stood. I wasn't going to end up in another situation where an arrogant doctor made me feel as if I didn't know any better.

"He's not allowed back in here. Ever."

Without me even having to explain what had transpired, she was already responding to my statement.

"Oh, that's just how he is. He is just very curt."

And that's an excuse, I thought to myself.

Jeffrey Dahmer. Yes, he eats people, but that's just how he is. He's very hungry.

Fuck that.

"I don't care." I am sure she was taken aback by my stance, but I wasn't going to bend. "He is not to step foot back in this room. Period."

Silence had gotten me nowhere but back into the hospital, and I was not going to make that mistake again.

I turned the television up to make sure she knew I was done with the conversation, and she silently left the room. Most likely to check with her charge nurse about protocol for refusing treatment from a surgeon, especially one that was scheduled to remove one of my chest tubes later that afternoon. It didn't matter. In my head, I was taking a stand for all of the patients who had been talked to like morons. Or treated like they weren't their own advocates. Or who wanted to punch a member of the medical staff square in the jaw but couldn't. Screw that guy.

Also, I kind of felt like a bad ass, standing up to a doctor. A win for nurses AND patients everywhere.

It was early that afternoon when the nurse practitioner returned to remove my chest tube. She was kind and personable, the exact kind of personality I wanted if I had to have someone yank a tube out of my chest. She made some small talk that included a veiled attempt to excuse her colleague's actions. I let it pass, as I felt like I had already said my piece and was benefiting from my stance.

There was minimal relief when she ripped (she was super gentle but 'ripped' is still a very accurate description) out the first tube. She mentioned that it was the smaller of the two tubes and it would be another few days before the larger one could be removed. I longed to be able to roll over and lie on my side, something I hadn't been able to do since all of this had started.

Add it to the list of "little things" that I wanted back in my life.

But don't worry, life was going to get really good for me, in a hot minute.

CHAPTER EIGHTEEN

The Wedding
September 1st, 2018

This whole story has been a lot. For me to relive. For you to read. I get it. But I promise, it wasn't all shitty. There were times that I laughed so hard I needed to wear my oxygen and times that I was so distracted by how happy I was that I got a brief moment of reprieve from feeling like the "sick" girl.

So how about a little reward for you all for sticking with me this long? I would say you deserve a little slice of happy amidst all of the bullshit, which is exactly what the wedding was. Of course, despite my attempts to completely forget, the wedding was not without reminders of LAM. I mean, it can't all be unicorns who shit out Skittles but, for the most part, the wedding was a beautiful break from what the last few years of my life had been.

When I went back to work after the Dominican, I remember just loving the feeling of living a regular life. I wasn't even mad that I was sitting in traffic for three hours each day because it meant that I had made it through the ordeal that everyone told me would "make a great book someday." Well, joke's on you guys because now I'm going to make you read it.

Sadly, our lives would suffer a couple more blows with the

loss of my grandmother, my first best friend, and the loss of Dan's father who was, quite possibly, one of the best people on the planet. I know we were both happy that we weren't attending my funeral, but it really would have been nice to hold on to those two family members for a bit longer.

I know, I said happy. I'm getting there.

Dan's father passed away around Thanksgiving and we had driven to New York and back in just a few days. The twelve-hour drive (one way) coupled with the emotional turmoil of the trip had left us exhausted and ready to sleep for days.

The night of our return, Dan and I sat in our kitchen.

"How are you feeling?" I asked. I know I knew the answer, but I wanted to say something. I wanted to try and break the silence; and any words strung together to form a sentence would have to do.

He didn't answer my question. Instead he said:

"My dad loved you."

"I know."

"I know you know, but I wanted to say it."

I smiled at him and took his hand. He hadn't cried much and I wasn't sure how he was truly handling things. So most of the time, I just let him say the things he felt he needed to and smiled so he knew I supported him.

Now, I cannot make this next part up. No matter what anyone else (Dan) tells you, this is exactly how this happened.

"You know," Dan said, getting up from the table, "it's going to be great to get married next year."

I tried not to look as taken aback as I was.

Yeah, that would be great, I thought as sarcastically as possible. If you would get off your ass and propose.

We had been together for five years and I had brought up marriage multiple times. He had become a master at evading any discussion that was centered around marriage to the point that I had given up on the idea. But perhaps he was being flippant.

I laughed. "Dan, you know, if we want to get married next year, we'd have to plan a wedding."

"Yeah."

He wasn't seeing the issue. I was going to have to be blunt.

"Dan. We have to be engaged before we plan a wedding." This felt like an overly obvious observation and yet, something told me that it needed to be said out loud.

I shit you not, this is what he said. Verbatim.

"Okay then, we're engaged."

I'm sorry, what in the fuck? He must have read my face because, without me saying anything at all, he took my face in his freckled hands, kissed my forehead, and said, "Yes. I'm serious."

He left the room. Literally, he said that and walked out of the room like something major hadn't just happened.

What in the *fuck*? (Yes, this recollection calls for two 'what in the fucks.')

I was engaged.

Question mark.

I felt like Charlotte on that episode of *Sex and the City* when she proposed to herself at dinner and her future ex-husband responded with "all-righty."

I had wanted to marry Dan since I was eighteen. I would show up at a concert, watch him play the guitar, and wait for the band to play "Brown Eyed Girl" so I could pretend he was singing it to me. But in all my fantasies, all of the scenarios I had envisioned, this was not how my engagement went down. It was almost clinical.

And yet, I was elated.

I was not sad there was no kneeling, I didn't care there was no flash mob, I wasn't even sad there wasn't a ring.

I was marrying Dan.

Like, for real.

I woke up the next morning as if it had been the grief or the booze talking. But almost immediately, he called me his fiancé, and we called our parents to let them know. The family and friend notifications would come after we picked out a ring; I had to have something to post on social media after all, or what was it all for?

After the ring came the planning. Neither of us wanted a long engagement—and by neither of us, I mean me. I had been planning our wedding since we started dating, so there was no need to dillydally. Yes, I said dillydally. And I stand by it. Move on.

There were flowers to choose. Dresses to buy. Money to spend.

There were guest lists to make. Venues to book.

Just like our trip to the Dominican, but obviously not as life-threatening, there was drama, because it's a wedding and of course everyone has an opinion. Just for the record, if it's not your wedding, all of your opinions are wrong. Keep that shit to yourself.

Even with all of the stress, and all of the nonsense, and all of the nights I told Dan we should just elope, there was a silver lining.

I wasn't thinking about LAM. For like, multiple days in a row. That was huge. I got to be a normal bride. Hell, I got to feel like a normal person. And everyone was going to be focused on me because I looked like an airbrushed queen and not because I almost died in a foreign country or because every doctor in the hospital wanted to meet the girl with the rare lung disease.

Nothing about my wedding had anything to do with my diagnosis and it was fucking glorious. Even with the pressure that comes with planning anything of this magnitude, I enjoyed the entire nine months leading up to our wedding.

The day of our wedding, it was supposed to rain. And not just an annoying drizzle, but a downpour.

Now, we have already established my nonexistent belief in a higher power, so I am certainly not going to say that some divine deity stopped the rain that day. However. Not one drop of rain fell. In fact, the weather was damn near perfect other than some wind that decided it wanted my veil to spend the majority of the ceremony in my face.

Dan looked like a fucking J. Crew model (seriously, it's upsetting how good he looked) and I was obsessed with my 1940s beaded gown. I bought the most expensive weave I could find, and it showed, and my sister made sure that my edges were on point (if you don't know what that means, ask one of your black girlfriends, but it's a big deal). My makeup was perfection and I felt absolutely beautiful.

It was the absolute perfect day.

I'm sorry.

That's a lie. But, you knew that, didn't you? I just wanted to use my rose-colored glasses for a second and remember that day being flawless and LAM-free.

Now, don't get me wrong. The day was happy. And beautiful. And I married the love of my life. I mean, even after he found out I was broken, he still chose me. He picked me. And we got married.

I, like many brides I'm sure, had a vision for not only the wedding, but how I wanted to spend the day.

But there was something that I wanted to do almost as much as I wanted to say those vows to Dan in front of our friends and family.

I wanted to dance at my wedding. Yes, with my husband during some slow and sappy song, but, more than that, I wanted to motherfucking dance. (Is that my first motherfucker? Wow. I'm classier than I thought.) I was going to be the bride that kicked off her heels, ran out, and Cha-Cha Slid. Or Wobbled. Or even Cotton-Eye Joed. I wanted to dance until the DJ was finished and they had to drag my champagne-laden ass off of the Formica dance floor.

But LAM still snuck in. Sneaky little bitch that she is.

I couldn't dance. Not in the Frank Sinatra metaphor kind of way, but I actually couldn't dance. I was able to shake my ass for the first two minutes of "No Diggity" before I felt like I was going to pass out from a lack of oxygen. (No doubt.)

I never said anything. I didn't even go cry in a bathroom stall like a girl who got dumped at prom, even though I wanted to. Because I certainly wasn't ungrateful. The day was amazing and it's not that I didn't relish marrying the love of my life. I mean, of course I did. And I loved almost everything about that day.

Except the not dancing. And the aforementioned drama. But, mostly the not dancing.

That's the thing with chronic illness, though; especially one so rare that loves to run rampant on your third most important organ. It doesn't give a shit if it's your wedding day. It's just there—sometimes sitting dormant just waiting to pop up and say, "Hey, remember me?"

But it's not all bad. Because even though I couldn't dance at my wedding, something that may seem trivial but was important to me, it was still the best day of my life (so far).

So, I guess that means that you really can learn to see through all of the mess, and the depression, and the anger, and enjoy the important moments for what they really are.

Important.

Look at me. Learning shit.

CHAPTER NINETEEN

The COVID-19
2020 and 2021 (and probably forever)

Some changes that happen after a diagnosis like LAM are obvious. Shortness of breath. Using oxygen. Fear of flying.

Annoying? Absolutely.

Unexpected. Not really.

And then there are the others. Let's call them "second-tier changes" because I like to name things so they sound fancy. These are the situations that I was unaware would occur, but after they happened could understand why they did. Things like changes in your family dynamic. The effects on your sex life (that's the chapter you better have skipped, Mom). The shift in your own personality.

Unexpected, but still eventually understood.

Not on either list? The effects of LAM when mixed with a global pandemic. To quote Sinead O'Connor, nothing compares to [COVID].

I imagine that if I wasn't sick, I would still have not been even remotely prepared for the dumpster fire that is (or was, depending) COVID-19, but I had no idea that having LAM would exponentially increase the physical and mental toll a global pandemic would already have on my life and the lives of people around me. (Side note: I realize that I sound like a broken record—constantly having epiphanies about how things that happen in my life affect the people I care about, but that's a topic for my therapist, not this book.)

Living during the COVID-19 pandemic has been an experience for everyone. But living during this time with LAM has been almost more difficult than any other hurdle I've had to clear. Even the Dominican. In fact, I would barely classify it as living; more like muddling through each day trying my best not to get drunk by noon.

Living with a rare disease (or any disease, I imagine) creates new experiences pretty regularly. They aren't necessarily the most fun experiences but, as I've said many times, they make a good story. What isn't quite as obvious are the events and circumstances that you aren't sure will affect you at all and then hit you like a brick wall.

That is COVID-19.

My appointment with my specialist in early March 2020 seemed like it would go as well as it possibly could. Lung function testing. An overly chipper nurse. And a review of my current medication regimen. I figured that it was going to be another run-of-the-mill appointment. For so long, every appointment that I went to came with bad news or shitty progress, or lungs that didn't want to cooperate. If things went well today, I'd have three appointments in a row where nothing happened.

And with LAM, nothing is everything.

My doctor and I shot the shit, joked around, and discussed the state of my lungs. Just as things were getting ready to wrap up, he said he had one more question.

"So, what are your feelings on COVID?"

I was taken aback by the question. Of course, I had heard of COVID-19, but my concern was minimal. Sure, it was serious, but I lived in a world of modern medicine. How concerned did I really have to be? The idea of it being an actual issue was barely in my periphery.

I took a beat, maybe less, and said, "Honestly, I'm not that concerned."

Without hesitation, he said, "Well, you should be."

Our witty banter had stopped and so had my flippant demeanor.

Cautious? Sure. But legitimately concerned? To be honest, I thought it seemed like a bit of an overreaction.

He went on to say that my fucked-up lungs (he may have said respiratory issues, but whatever) and my medication and its immunosuppressing effects put me at high risk for both contracting COVID-19 and becoming seriously ill as a result. He told me I needed to take things extremely seriously and that he would keep me posted on things as they progressed.

I left the appointment feeling more lost than I had in a while. I had finally reached a place in my treatment and diagnosis where I felt like I was on the other side of all of the shitty things that had happened over the past few years. My appointments had become less regular; always a good thing when it comes to disease monitoring. It was also just me at my doctors' appointments these days; no Angie, no Dan, no Mom. Just me on my own to take in the information without the codependence of the tribe I had leaned on for so much of this. I had learned to trust my doctors with my life (literally) and I had stopped feeling scared every single day.

His words seemed to suck all of that progress out of my head, despite the years it took to get me there. The last thing I wanted was one more unknown. Was I annoyed? Of course. Was I scared? Maybe a little. Did I have any idea that 2020 would end up being my second "impossible year?" Not in the slightest.

The coming months would prove to be a true test of my strength (or lack thereof), my relationship, and my overall mental (in)stability.

To quote Ron Burgundy, what happened in the coming weeks "escalated quickly."

In a matter of days, I went from working at a hospital full time, to working intermittently from home, to "being at home for the foreseeable future."

Foreseeable. Future.

Never comforting to hear. Especially when uncertainty had seemed to be the only constant in my life for so long. I was more uneasy than I was at the start, yet I was still okay. Sure, it wasn't the ideal situation, but if the worst of it was having to work from home for a while, I felt like I was ahead of the curve.

But, as we know now, that was not the worst of it.

The second week of March was spent working from my house and creating power point presentations that focused on the COVID-19 initiatives being put into place. Perhaps that should have been a large clue. The government had yet to seem terribly concerned about what COVID-19 meant for the U.S. population, but the medical community was ramping up for something major. I'm embarrassed now that I didn't see the signs, but even with a medical background, the idea of a pandemic seemed like an archaic concept.

I was wrong.

So many of us were wrong.

In 2020, my last day out of the house for the next 300-plus days was March 15th.

Losing the ability to socially interact hit swiftly, and it hit hard. While I had come a long way from the girl who was out and about with friends nonstop, I still enjoyed the occasional night out or therapeutic shopping excursion. Unfortunately, the risk of contracting COVID did not outweigh the benefit of social interaction and so I said goodbye to that piece of my life. I also said goodbye to my job; the call from my doctor informing me of my quarantine came as I was leaving work on a rainy Tuesday afternoon.

"Hi, Dr. Hewlett," I said.

"It's time for you to quarantine. I'm so sorry." He meant it,

I could tell.

"But my job..." Surely, he would tell me I could keep my job as long as I stayed safe.

I could not. Apparently, all hospitals were unsafe for me, even the ones that only treated psychiatric patients. I had only been in my hospital-based role for six months and I hadn't even mentioned my diagnosis because "what could possibly happen?" What in hell was I going to tell them?

While my mind raced, my doctor continued to explain the situation and the importance of maintaining a very strict house arrest. "You have to stay in your house. For the foreseeable future. Again, I'm so sorry."

He hung up. Or I did. I don't think either of us knew what else to say.

For the foreseeable future. There were those words again. Although the phrase hit a little harder this time.

Second to go after my freedom, and possibly the most difficult, was my marriage. Not in the sense of our love for each other, but in the sense of what made us a couple and not just roommates. Dan continued to work and while his interaction with people was minimal, it was still a part of his day-to-day existence. As a result, the safest decision to make was to remain at a six-foot distance as much as possible. We stopped hugging, stopped kissing, and stopped sleeping in the same bed. It was very much a War of the Roses situation, sans the mansion and disdain for each other. Our marriage was operating at 25% capacity through no fault of our own and the results on my mental health were palpable.

The only thing worse than missing someone is missing someone who is standing right in front of you. We had made it through so much and instead of enjoying normalcy, we were being forced to live two separate lives. Illogical as it was, there were days I would have risked COVID-19 just to get back to feeling like I could enjoy being a newlywed.

The third thing to go was my job. For the first three weeks

of my quarantine, I was able to work from home and feel like I had some semblance of a routine. But being a nurse in a time of medical panic means that job functions shift and non-bedside nursing goes to the wayside. So, as a nurse, I was needed, probably more than I'll ever see again in my career. On the flip side, being immunocompromised, specifically, being a LAM patient, meant that I was high risk, and being high risk meant that it was not safe for me to be in a hospital setting.

As a nurse, I felt useless. As a person, I felt even more useless. The nurse portion of me wanted to be on the front lines and the person portion of me just wanted to feel like a functioning member of society. It's one thing to be out of work when you don't feel well; it's another thing to feel good but be forced to furlough because your body is fighting itself.

Once again, the three horsemen of misery-pocalypse reared their ugly heads.

I felt guilty.

I felt depressed.

I felt alone.

I had beat out multiple applicants for my position, including some internal candidates. I don't say that to brag, but to make a point about how important it was that I prove myself. And yet, two months in, the position was once again vacant. My head told me to resign. To allow someone else to perform the job they had waited so long to fill. I imagined the conversations about my being there barely long enough for people to know my name before I disappeared with almost no notice.

And then, the final straw. A call from HR requesting I apply for short-term disability because "pandemic pay just wasn't appropriate."

"It's not like you're sick," the rep who must have had a death wish said to me over the phone. "I mean, you don't actually *have COVID*, so you really shouldn't be getting pandemic pay."

That phone call resulted in one of my biggest emotional

breakdowns to date. And I don't say that lightly. In my normal day-to-day life, I cry. A lot. Almost daily. Even before LAM, I was always the one who had the most emotional reaction to things. I cry because I'm happy, because I'm sad, because I'm angry, and because it's Tuesday.

I cry at the end of *The Green Mile* every time I watch it as if I don't know the ending.

I cry because I wonder if the old man in the Walmart commercial is a widower.

This (over) reaction was nothing like any of those times.

I could barely breathe when I called my husband and told him I was officially on disability. I. Was. Not. Disabled. I was a thirty-eight-year-old woman who worked her ass off for her career and finally felt like she was going somewhere.

I wasn't a patient.

I wasn't post-surgery.

I just needed to be somewhere safe.

Everything was as it was, only I finally had to admit that even on my best days, LAM made every other part of my life abnormal.

I knew he didn't know what to say. The words "everything will be fine" seemed empty to both of us at this point. I tried to hang up the phone before he felt like he had to say something.

What in the fuck was I going to do?

Some number of months and some more pounds later...

I spent nine months watching old reruns of *ER* on Hulu, making sure that everyone I knew had watched the *Tiger King* at least twice, memorizing the words (and re-enacting scenes) from *Hamilton*, and counting how many steps it was from my kitchen back to the couch. (It was nine.) I became increasingly angry at the people who were able to do more than stare at the same four walls all day. I was mad at the people who weren't taking things as seriously as I was, all the time knowing that without LAM, I would likely be one of them.

I could not begin to count how many times I cried, how sad I became, and how quickly I regressed to a place of no fucks given, even after all I had been through. How quickly I became the person Dan once described as "not who I used to be." Except this time, I was painfully aware.

As much as I hated when people would tell me "it can always be worse," I knew that it could be. Yet, I wallowed in it. I thrived off of my self-pity and used it to fuel all of my anger.

I was gross. Like, really gross.

Until something random, hilarious, and beautiful happened. It was the first moment during quarantine I remember feeling any other way than melancholy. It happened so randomly I didn't even have time to think about anything else. I forgot about the crumbling world around me and laughed (at someone else's expense, of course) until I thought I was going to have to put my oxygen on.

I do not have a way to preface this story that isn't clunky or odd, so just insert your own witty segue here. I can't do *all* of the work for you.

I ignored most of my phone calls during COVID-19—more so than I do when the world is normal which, if you ask anyone who knows me, happens pretty regularly. (The hierarchy is text, FaceTime, telegram, yelling into a void, then phone call; just so you have the information.) The calls I accepted were few and far between, mostly because I had nothing to say. On this night, I broke my rule and answered the phone. What followed was a ten-minute period of laughing until I cried; something my psyche desperately needed.

My phone rang and on the other end was a girlfriend in a complete panic. I could hear it in her voice and my heart immediately skipped a beat. What horrible thing had happened that warranted a call at 10:00 p.m. on a Tuesday (not that I had anything better to do)?

In the background, I heard a faint noise, but I was unable

to make it out.

"Jesus Christ, Sara, I'm having a crisis."

Fuck.

What in hell was wrong? Did she catch COVID? Did her kid? Was everyone okay? I suddenly felt our 2,000-mile gap as I planned out in my head how I would get out to her if I needed. I didn't need to. All I needed to do was listen to what came out of her mouth next.

"I can't shut off my vibrator."

Suddenly, the familiarity of the sound I was hearing became glaringly obvious. In the background was the steady hum of a small- to medium-sized vibrator. (It's not important why I know, so let's just move on. Perverts.) She had clearly placed it in a box and I listened to her breathing pattern increase as she ran around her house trying to find a place to put it.

I could feel the laughter welling up; it was like being in church and being told you can't laugh. I could barely get the next sentence out. "Just take the batteries out, you ass."

"I can't," she said. "It doesn't have batteries. I wanted to be green."

At that point, my suppressed laughter came bellowing out of my mouth. I had no words, no advice. Just an endless loop of laughter as I thought about my friend running around her house trying to find a place to hide her malfunctioning vibrator where it wouldn't be heard by the rest of her family. I had no idea how much I needed to laugh until I cried, until it happened. Granted, it was at the expense of my friend, who had clearly called for my help, but I knew she would understand.

That was the exact moment I realized that everything was going to be okay. While the pandemic had increased my depression, alcohol intake, and waist size, it had not affected my ability to laugh with a friend (and let's be honest, *at* her a little bit too). It was at this point that I knew, when all was said and done, none of this was permanent. And that, once again, I would come out on the other side of a crisis with the core of my personality still intact.

The pandemic didn't end at this moment, nor did my depression and feelings of uncertainty.

(Or my abundance of alcohol and carbohydrate consumption.)

But the "vibrator incident" did more than just provide for a silly anecdote in an otherwise depressing chapter. It showed me that I could still come out on the other side with a sense of humor, positivity, and maybe, eventually, a little less liquor consumption.

So, to that friend, I'm sorry about your vibrator.

But not really. Because I really needed that laugh. Probably more than she needed her vibrator to shut itself off.

Without knowing it, her crisis had reminded me that even with LAM, even after the Dominican Republic, even after COVID-19 and an endless quarantine, I always seemed to make it out of the storm. Not totally unscathed, but certainly not defeated.

CHAPTER TWENTY

The Gym(s)

For the sake of staying with me, as I assume you have since you are this far along, I need you to trust me when I say this particular chapter is an important piece of this janky puzzle. Going to a gym is a trivial thing to so many people, but I would be doing this story a disservice if I did not acknowledge how the simple act of exercise was an integral part of my "journey."

Let me address one thing out of the gate.

I have NEVER been a gym person. Like ever.

Ask my friends. Old and new. Because my hatred of gyms was a lifestyle.

In fact, I was obnoxiously anti any exercise. I had no desire to devote any sort of physical exertion to get from point A to point B. I would not be walking, skiing, jumping, swimming, jogging, biking, or curling my happy ass anywhere.

And that says a lot, because I fucking love curling.

In the times I was forced to run (thank you, high school presidential fitness test), I was not the person who ever experienced a runner's high. I remember getting peer pressured into attending a Cross Fit class in my mid-twenties that ended with me vomiting in the parking lot and then going out for nachos. There was never a part of me that felt like the gym would be something constant, let alone an enjoyable and fulfilling experience.

You may wonder what the gym has to do with LAM, let alone an entire chapter. But it does so, as you have so far, bear with me.

I started going to the gym after the Dominican at the recommendation of my doctor. "Nothing too crazy," she said, just walking on the treadmill to help build my lung function. Little did she know that even that level of exercise sounded like misery to me.

But I would do it—because my fear of death trumped my loathing of the gym; even if it was just barely.

So, here is something they don't tell you—and by "they," I mean anyone.

Likely because when it happens, it really isn't considered anything substantial by most. Maybe because it doesn't happen to everyone, or maybe even because it shouldn't be considered a negative.

But I hated it. It made a lump swell up in my throat and I wanted to crawl into a hole and pull it in after me.

The first time it happened, I was walking on the treadmill, incline high, oxygen tubing shoved up my nose, listening to what I can only assume was '90s hip-hop or a carefully selected compilation of Broadway songs. Out of the corner of my eye, I thought I saw an older gentleman walking towards me. That being said, I was in a gym and in the direct path of the exit, so there was certainly a possibility I was being paranoid.

Good chance he was not walking towards, but past.

But he kept heading my way and eventually we locked eyes. Yup.

He was definitely headed towards. Fucking fuck.

He stopped in front of my treadmill and smiled at me. Not in a weird creepy way. Not in an old-man-with-a-fetish-for-black-girls kind of way. It was kind. I could tell by his eyes. His reasons, whatever they were, were not ill-intentioned. That was part of the reason I still feel like such a shit for harboring bad feelings for someone whose only intention was to make sure I knew that he thought I was doing something amazing.

But I did. And I do; still hate some random old man who was just trying to be nice.

When he remained standing in front of me despite my clear attempt to avoid a conversation, I reluctantly removed my headphones and smiled back.

"Hi," I said. "Did you need this machine?" I didn't think that was the case since I was flanked with empty treadmills on either side of me, but I couldn't imagine what else he possibly had to say.

He looked at me, with his smile and his kind eyes, and said, "You're an inspiration. Keep it up."

He didn't wait for a response, just turned and walked out of the gym.

This is where I become aware that I sound a bit crazy. But just hear me out.

It was in that moment that I realized that my oxygen made me look sick. Without it, I looked like a "normal" and healthy woman, but with it, I was a young-ish looking girl who needed help to breathe. While in my day-to-day life, there was nothing about me that would lead people to think I was nothing but healthy, my oxygen was like a big scarlet "O" on my chest, letting the world know there was something wrong with me.

I didn't want to be an inspiration.

Hell. It seemed like lately, I could barely muster up the strength to be a decent human being.

I just didn't want to die. (Thus, the oxygen.)

A comment that was meant to be kind instead ended up being something that played on an endless loop in my head, reminding me how abnormal my life had become. And it happened all the time. But, for some reason, it bothered me most in the gym. Likely because I'm sure the people who wanted to pray for me, or thought I was some sort of inspiration, had no clue that every single time someone felt the need to make a comment, I felt the sudden urge to punch them in the face.

I didn't. Because that's not nice. Or legal.

So instead, I utilized all of my energy by making sure I smiled. And said thank you. And acted like the words didn't grate every last nerve I had left. More often than not, it was enough for them to offer me one more "go get 'em, tiger" look before they left me alone with my thoughts and whatever random playlist I happened to be listening to that day.

After the first encounter, I went to the gym for a couple more months. More often than not, someone would smile, give me a thumbs-up, or tell me that I should "keep it up."

You keep it up.

I got to the point where I felt like I was an exhibit at a zoo. It seemed like no one could walk by the girl with the tubing and not think to themselves, "that poor thing." I hated every part about being in that big open space, on display with my shitty lungs and my little oxygen backpack. Hell, I didn't even have the benefit of experiencing that gym high I've heard so much about.

And I'm stubborn. So stubborn in fact that, despite the realization that my breathing had, in fact, improved, and that I had come to only slightly dislike the mundane nature of a thirty-minute walk on a treadmill, I stopped going to the gym. If I wasn't wearing my oxygen, I could compartmentalize my diagnosis and tuck it neatly into the catacombs of my brain. I could pretend that I was normal; that my life was normal. Or at least some of my life was normal.

At least it would stop the looks of pity and prayers from strangers that gave me abdominal pain.

So, I stuffed my oxygen into the back of a closet, and quit the gym.

I was okay with it for a while. I didn't feel better about myself, but oddly, I didn't feel worse either.

* * * * * * *

I found myself, sometime later, discussing my lack of exercise with a friend. She casually mentioned her gym and said I should check it out. I laughed; I can't remember if it was in my head or out loud, but it was probably the latter, because I knew which gym she went to.

You want me to go to a gym that has "Boot Camp" in its name? You must be out of your 7% body fat mind.

There is no way I was going to fit in at this gym, let alone get to a point where I didn't loathe the thought of spending forty-five minutes a day working out. Not to mention, I pictured a bunch of fit upper middleclass women who would take one look at my body and oxygen backpack and wonder if I'd gotten lost on the way to Waffle House or Ross Dress for Less. I could barely handle the low bar that had been set for me at the previous gym; hell, all it took was several thoughts and prayers to get me to hang up my Nikes.

And yet, somehow, she convinced me.

"Just try it," she said. "Trust me."

Now. Pay attention to this next part. Because there is a good chance I have never uttered the following words and an even better chance I will never say them again. Seriously. Ask anyone who knows me. I do not say the next three words often.

So. Here goes.

I was wrong.

(Just typing that out made me throw up in my mouth a little bit.)

But I was. And I've never been happier about it.

It's hard to explain why this gym worked when the others didn't, especially without sounding like you are trying to get someone to join a cult. I think I got close once when I was asked to write my story for the gym's website. And I don't think there is anything more poignant than what I wrote down in that moment. It was certainly not the most articulate thing I've ever put to paper, but it may be one of the most honest.

"What I found in Burn was a group of women who cared about not only my health, but me as an individual. I had let the fear of being defined by my disease, and the oxygen that came along with it, nearly allow me to miss out on becoming a member of one of the greatest communities I have ever been a part of. I always thought oxygen would be my crutch. Instead, my oxygen is what got me to Burn."

It sounds sappy as hell and maybe even a little made up, but it's the truth. I had no idea what I was missing—and it wasn't about not wanting to work out. Hell, it wasn't even about the thoughts and prayers; it was about feeling proud of myself. And not feeling singled out. Sure, there were times I would get a glance from a friend who wanted to make sure I was okay if I looked like my oxygen was dipping, but more often than not, I was just Sara. And just so you don't think I've totally changed, I *do* get just a twinge of satisfaction when a new person comes in and can't keep up with the girl on oxygen.

I mean, let's face it; that is pretty fucking cool.

I'm not an inspirational poster and I'm certainly not a role model. I never will be and frankly, I don't want that kind of pressure. I'm not even the reason you should get off your ass and go to the gym; whatever that means to you. I'm not the reason you should do anything unless that thing is letting yourself be just a little vulnerable and getting out of a thirty-year-old comfort zone. Maybe not a leap out of the comfort zone, but just a jump to the left.

The point of this is certainly not to peer pressure you to join a gym because I think that it will magically transform you into a better person. It's not like I went to the gym and suddenly became some sort of saint. Hell, I didn't even get to the point where I could exercise without oxygen, which was the original goal all those months ago.

But, what did happen was this: somehow, this gym saw

me deep in the throes of my anger, chaos, and uncertain life, and managed to make me smile.

Wearing oxygen.

While doing burpees.

And that says something.

CHAPTER TWENTY-ONE

The Shit I Lost (And Gained)

It is my belief that during a health crisis, most people experience loss that goes beyond the decrease in physicality and lack of a healthy body. Sure, that is the most obvious measure of functional decline, but after that comes a series of both expected and unexpected losses. It truly is a domino effect that seems to be never-ending and, in my case, I lose things almost regularly; some more obvious than others.

I know several women who mourned the loss of their hair when undergoing chemotherapy; something that many women (including myself) attribute to beauty. I've certainly grieved the loss of the things I discussed earlier; lung function and motherhood. I think those two losses are global—I think most women, disease or no disease, would understand what it would be like to have motherhood snatched from you like your purse in a New York City subway.

And while both of those experiences nearly broke me, the loss of my ability to sing shattered much of the hope I had left; mostly because it was truly such a major part of who I was and who I am even still. Now, pardon me if Alanis has ruined my ability to clearly identify proper irony, but I believe I've got this right:

I'm a singer with a debilitating and progressive lung disease.

(It's like raaaaaaaaaaaaiiiiiinn...)

Just kidding.

But seriously. I'm a singer by definition; and it's a combination of my love for music, my love of the craft, and for my years spent executing my instrument. When I was five, I had the lead in the play and I had the first solo of the show. I soaked up every moment of being on the stage, in front of the entire school, and singing my heart out. I can't picture myself in a world where my voice is gone and only the memories of performing are left. And yet, that has become a real and horrifying possibility.

Honestly, when everything started, I didn't even think about losing the ability to sing. If I had, I don't know if I'd have survived. Literally. It's that important to me. Being a good...

You know what, no. This is not the time for modesty. Let me rephrase.

Being a *great* singer was who I was. It defined me in a way that made me proud. And I loved when people asked if I was the girl with the voice.

Fuck yes, I was.

I'm sure it goes back further, but it wasn't until high school that I began to realize I had the potential to be really good at something. I was never good at sports. I fucked around playing clarinet in the band, but it was mostly because it was a requirement in elementary school. I even tried to be an artist for a very messy few months. But nothing came as natural or brought me as much joy as singing. I joined the chorus freshman year of high school, like every good nerd does, and I never looked back.

I was an average singer at the start—nothing to write home about. I, like most girls, thought that in order to be a good singer,

I had to be a soprano. The Sopranos (capitalized here on purpose) are a bossy and elite group of women who basically run any choir they are a part of (ask them, they'll tell you). I wasn't a bad soprano, but I certainly wasn't a natural one.

My sophomore year of high school, a new choir director brought with her a different vision of what the chorus should look and sound like; including making me an alto.

An alto.

The worst.

Suddenly, I was going from rocking the notes in the rafters to singing the same note over and over again while the sopranos (and sometimes the tenors) got all of the accolades. I had never felt so insulted and small in my life.

Turns out, that was my game changer.

Not only was I truly an alto, but I was also a belter (something that was much less prevalent and sought after than it is now). I thought singing made me happy before, but once I found my true voice, singing gave me a feeling that can only be described as orgasmic.

I parlayed my love of singing into an absolute adoration of musical theater. I loved nothing more than being on stage. I craved the applause of an audience like a junkie craved heroin and crossed my fingers for a standing ovation during my final bow.

After my diagnosis, I didn't notice an immediate decline in my ability to sing. And, as funny as it is, the idea that could be a result didn't cross my mind. I suppose it was partly due to how much I had on my plate—thinking you are going to die does take up a good amount of space in your brain.

Even after all the surgeries, even after starting oxygen, I remained oblivious that LAM would continue to take some of the most important things I had away from me.

It wasn't until I decided it was time for me to get back on stage that it became glaringly obvious after an audition that happened in early 2019. After searching since my move in 2013, I had found a community theater group in Nashville (there are less than you'd think) and they were auditioning for *Avenue Q*, a show that was a perfect fit for me.

I walked into the audition that evening confident in my abilities, but forgetting that I had not attempted a solo singing performance since my diagnosis. My name was the first name called, and I handed the pianist my sheet music, ready to belt out my song. Instead, after only seconds, my lungs felt like they were going to explode. The more I pushed, the worse I felt.

It was almost reminiscent of those post-surgery days when it felt as if breathing would never come naturally again.

It seems LAM took my lungs and with it, my stamina, which directly affected my voice. Sitting and singing was no issue as was obvious during auditions but, the minute I tried to incorporate any movement while I sang, I quickly lost my breath, became dizzy, and was unable to sing more than two or three notes at a time. (I still got the part though.)

After that first night of rehearsal, I cried in my car the entire way home. Literally hyperventilated while I drove down the interstate singing along to my "inspiration songs" playlist between sobs. I was back on stage but far from 100%. My voice was strong but my stage presence was going to take a hit. And who wants to watch a chubby girl belt out a tune while she just stands in one spot. Boring. Singing and performing had become who I was. I had worked my ass off to be considered good, even great. That night, driving home, all that kept running through my head was that LAM had stolen my skill, my talent, my heart, and my twenty years of hard work.

It chewed it up, spit it out, and then told it to fuck off.

LAM made me mediocre.

I wanted to quit the show. I had visions of being laughed at and people wondering how the hell I got the part in the first place. I no longer felt like the girl who could effortlessly belt out songs and make it look easy. I felt like some sort of imposter. I was mad at LAM for a lot of things; but this one hit harder than any other. LAM waited until I wasn't expecting it, and then kicked me right in the balls.

Now, I realize that sounds a tad melodramatic.

But I am a theater person, after all. I thrive when I'm submerged in drama.

But I bottled it up, stuck it in the recesses of my brain, and pretended it wasn't the truth. I went through with the show and, while I had one of the best times of my life, I still wish that I had been able to perform like I had even five years before.

I likely mentioned in passing that I was frustrated with the state of my singing (in)ability, but I never told anyone how truly devastated I was. Mostly because I didn't want to pretend I was comforted by the generic phrases like...

"There's more to you than your voice."

Or

"At least you have your health."

Or

"You sound just like you used to."

I wasn't quite sure what to do with my feelings. It's not like there's a support group for singers who were okay, but then got really good, and then got a rare lung disease, and then weren't as good (or maybe they were and it was all in their head) and really just want to cry about it and then scream into a pillow.

I mean, the acronym alone would be ridiculous.

I also didn't want to sound full of myself. I have never actually said out loud that I believed myself to be a great singer. But I did. Or maybe I still do?

There is a good chance that, even though I can't sing as many notes in a row as I used to, and that I'll never get the chance to play Velma Kelly (which would have been a stretch anyway), the core of my voice is still there. And maybe it's not as obvious to everyone else that I am running out of breath at a rapid rate and trailing off at the end of phrases. Or maybe it is and it doesn't matter nearly as much as I think it does.

Regardless, in my head it was one more loss.

It was one more thing I had to mourn, long before I would have had to otherwise.

* * * * * * *

Alright. Time for some positivity. (I know, it's been sparse, but bear with me. I promise it won't be too sappy and gross.)

LAM didn't take *everything* away from me; it would be melodramatic to say so, in addition to being untrue. While I can associate a lot (and I mean a fucking LOT) of negative life experiences to LAM, there are also positives to it that go beyond a Facebook page and a gym membership (not that those are trivial things by any means).

First, I buried a lot of hatchets. And I mean a lot.

I hold a grudge like, well, a Taurus. And if astrology isn't your thing but you know my mother, I hold a grudge like she does. After my diagnosis, or maybe I should say after I came to terms with my diagnosis, I did my best to let go of petty grudges. I even managed to let go of some grudges that I felt were (and still are) completely justified.

"Some" being the operative word. I still keep a grudge or two on hand for a rainy day.

I had lost touch with several people who had been great friends to me at one time or another for reasons I wasn't even able to verbalize. In doing so, I got relationships back that I had no idea how much I really missed. I can't say that I never would have made the effort, had I not been diagnosed, but I am pretty sure I would not have been so quick to forgive and forget.

Make no mistake, I can still hold a grudge (or even choke the shit out of one) for the right reasons, but at least I know that I'm no longer missing pieces of people's lives who played such a large role in mine.

Along the same vein, I got better at creating realistic boundaries. Not that there were many people in my life that didn't belong there; but a handful of them had, for one reason or another, reached a point where they were offering me nothing but anxiety and one more excuse to crack open a bottle of Jack Daniel's at 1:30 p.m. on a Wednesday. My relationship issues went far beyond the petty grudges I held near and dear to my heart at one point or another.

These people truly had to go; for both of our sakes. And I drew those lines. Perhaps sloppily and not in the most articulate fashion, but they were drawn. I stopped worrying about what the repercussions of setting boundaries would do to the people on the outskirts of the situation, and instead I thought about how my life...

...my SHORTENED life...

...would be much more enjoyable surrounded by people who weren't passive-aggressive, narcissistic, cruel, hurtful, selfish jerks.

The racists, the homophobes, the Bible-thumping hypocrites (and honestly, just hypocrites in general) all had to go. No matter how long they had been in my life and no matter who they were. And goddamn, did it feel good to cut those ties.

And I was right. And some of those people weren't easy to remove for one reason or another. But the repair of friendships past and the removal of douche bags present made me hopeful for whatever future I had.

This next gain is my favorite. The relationship that became so much more after my diagnosis that I want to go back and have from the jump. My sister. My best friend. And not in that unrealistic way that the Disney Channel portrays where two sisters have been best friends since the beginning of time even though they were complete opposites. Because, and she will tell you the same, we were not always best friends.

Hell, there was a time we were barely acquaintances.

I'm pretty sure there was a point in time we tried to punch

each other in the parking lot of a community college; but she can write *that* book.

Now we talk every day. And I get to call her my best friend. Which is something amazing. Is it because she has kids now? Maybe. But I also know that there hasn't been a time since my diagnosis that I have gone more than a day or two without hearing her voice. And I had no idea how much I needed that, until I had it.

And lastly, my relationship with my husband has changed; mostly because he literally saved my life. But more than that, I have realized that we have a bond on a different level because of LAM. He's the man who talked to me about having children before we had even been together long enough to think about getting a dog, let alone having a baby. He's the man who didn't leave, even when I told him to. And even when he thought I was going to die in a developing nation (which I only found out recently), he never let me see him scared.

We're not perfect, but we have something just a little extra. LAM did that.

Edit: I would like to apologize for the gooey sappiness that is the end of this chapter. I feel like I need to include something extra. Can I interest you in a rogue profanity?

Fuck.

There. That feels better.

CHAPTER TWENTY-TWO

The End(?)

Here we are.

The point where I realize there is nothing important left to say. At least not on this topic.

When I began writing, my hope was that by the time I was ready to finish, I would experience some cathartic conclusion that would wrap everything up nicely and leave the reader (and myself) with some sort of grand life lesson. It certainly didn't help that whenever I told people I was writing a book, I got some version of "well, what's the point of it?" in their litany of questions.

I began to wonder the same. What *was* the point? When I could not answer that question, I stopped writing. For quite a while, actually. Sure, part of that was a lack of motivation, but most of it stemmed from the realization that perhaps I had nothing to say. That this was more like the diary of a diagnosis scorned and not what I would consider a book with a beginning, middle, and end.

Still, I wanted to be able to offer something. A moral. Or a lesson. Or a purpose. Even if it was super vague and cliché.

"Hey everyone, look what I learned."

"Look how much I've changed for the better."

"Look at how I've grown."

"If I can do it, you can do it."

"My disease does not define me."

"I have figured out the true meaning of life."

"I believe in God again."

None of those epiphanies came and when that moment didn't happen, I was, once again, at a loss; a feeling that was becoming all too comfortable taking up residence in my head. It was clear I had changed since my diagnosis, but not to a point where I felt like I had something wise to offer the masses. I certainly didn't write a book on proper coping skills, or how not to push people away in times of crisis, or how to avoid developing and maintaining a drinking problem in your thirties.

Then again, there was a chance I was overthinking. I admit, I am that person who needs everything tied up in a neat little package in order to feel fulfilled. It's why I don't watch *Unsolved Mysteries*, why I was never going to be an ER nurse; why a song can NEVER end on the seventh (if you know, you know).

For me, the conclusion is the resolve—and without resolve, you're just left in some sort of weird emotional purgatory.

No, thank you.

Without an ending, what's the point?

What was all of this for?

And then it hit me. In the middle of the night, while I should have been sleeping, but instead was wide-awake listening to Keith Morrison explain why it wasn't actually an ordinary night. I was overwhelmed with the realization that there was literally no end in sight.

But that's it.

That IS the point.

A conclusion doesn't define an experience. It just makes the experience more justifiable, and easier to deal with. Especially when it's a difficult one.

But, this is not about that. All this time I thought it was, and I could not have been more wrong.

(See, Dan, I actually CAN admit when I'm wrong.)

It's about all the shit that happened in the middle. All of the raw emotions, and poorly handled reactions, and the development of bad habits and an increased alcohol tolerance. It's about mourning the losses, and celebrating the gains even though sometimes it feels as if the gains will never come or are so few and far between that they feel meaningless. It's about remembering that even with all of your shitty behavior, you have a ride-or-die crew that has stopped you from jumping off a bridge. Likely on more than one occasion.

As sappy and cliché as it sounds, I hope that someone reads this and feels heard. Maybe even a little less alone.

This is for the people like me; the people with that rare disease, or even just a difficult diagnosis in general. Maybe even those people who had an unexpected event cause their lives to do a complete one-eighty.

It's also for the people who live every day of their life without resolution; the people who feel like every time they have learned to cope, something new crops up. That may be because of a diagnosis, or it may be because of something I've never experienced.

This is for all of you who spend your days riding with your mortality in the passenger seat. And let me tell you, that fucker is one chatty traveling companion.

I want you to know that your crazy, irrational, and sometimes psychotic behavior is all okay. In moderation, of course. (I'm still working on the moderation piece myself.)

I want you to understand the passing of time does not necessarily mean you will always feel healed; that you won't have days when the world seems to be crushing down on you. I don't know who said this originally, but they were wrong; time does not heal all wounds—just some of them. It all depends on how deep they were to begin with.

I want you to know that I see you when all you want to do is throw a four-year-old level temper tantrum and scream "It's not fair!" while you hold your breath and stomp your feet.

And that it's okay when you do.

And that it really isn't fair.

And when it comes to your diagnosis, sometimes knowing you never get to say the two words "I'm better" can be more devastating than the diagnosis itself.

That you love your friends and family but still wish at least one of them could sympathize instead of empathize. And knowing that immediately after you have that thought, you feel ungrateful for having it.

That you think of death on an extremely regular basis—more often than anyone at such a young age should be thinking about it. And that it terrifies you because even as an adult, you have an irrational (or hell, a completely rational) fear of dying too early.

That it's okay for you to mourn the life you could have had.

That the cost of being sick far surpasses the cost of being healthy, and it's okay to say it's not fair. Because it isn't.

That it's also okay to get angry when people flippantly try to justify the decisions you had to make that were out of your control.

That you should go to therapy; consistently. And that finding that therapist that gets it could mean all the difference.

That when you call in sick to work because you are so consumed with crushing sadness and depression, it doesn't make you weak. It just makes you human.

That some people don't get it. And it's not your job to explain it to them.

That you will have days when you feel so alone it scares you.

That you think about your mortality far more than you should; and that your fear of dying is rational and okay. We don't all handle death with ease.

That no matter your diagnosis, no matter your prognosis, no matter how many times you cycle through that fucking grief model, that someone, somewhere is experiencing life in parallel.

Am I still angry? Abso-fucking-lutely.

Do I sometimes cry because I get out of breath climbing three or four stairs?

I sure as shit do.

Do I feel like my mortality continues to ride shotgun most days?

Yup.

Does it feel as crushing as it did in the beginning? Not so much.

There is a chance that some of these feelings may never go away, but hopefully they become more of an ensemble character and less of a starring role. And if they don't, maybe I've actually learned some coping skills that don't involve getting drunk and crying in a bathroom.

I can say that right now, as I write these last words, it's somewhere in between; a recurring character but not a series regular.

And to the people who tell me that I am not the person I was before, they are 100% correct. But, I don't take those words as a slight anymore.

Am I great? Nope.

But I am okay. And being okay feels like everything I need right now.

And, one more thing. If you've made it this far, and if even one thing I said resonated, please know this:

I see you.

I feel you.

I know it sucks.

And sometimes, I hate it here too.

ACKNOWLEDGEMENTS

Only with the support and guidance from the following groups and individuals was *Gasping for Air* possible.

My mother and sister, of course. Thank you for loving me, even when I made it difficult. Thank you for keeping me going when I wanted to give up, and for being with me every step of the way. Without you, there would be no story to tell.

Dan, the love of my life. Thank you for more than I could ever articulate but mostly, for being the one who stayed even after I told you to leave.

Angie S., Jason R., and Nicole A., thank you for starting the Go Fund Me even though you knew I'd be mad about it, for calling the embassy, and all of the other behind the scenes work you did to get me home.

Erin M., my first editor. Thank you for the hours of work you poured into my manuscript, and for helping me realize the true potential of my story. And, of course, for rating me a six out of ten on a scale of political incorrectness.

Sarah M., Cheryl F., Beth, P., Kelsey D., Michelle C., Tim L., and Caren, D. thank you for reading countless versions of this book, for keeping me honest, and for telling me to keep going. And for correcting my questionable grammar.

To the 'Lammies,' you all have no idea what you have meant for me and my sanity. You made me feel seen and heard, all without judgement. I am so thankful for you and the entire LAM community. If I had to get diagnosed with a rare disease, I'm glad it was one with such supportive and amazing group of women.

Atmosphere Press, thank you for taking a longshot on a non-published author and for all of your support throughout the publishing process.

And finally, to all of you who donated to the GoFundMe all those years ago. I am forever grateful for your generosity, your support, your kindness, and for all of you helping to save my life. Thank you will never be enough.

Dave and Barb L., Robin T., Nyanda D., Robyn E., The Millis Family, Luke K., Deb N., Kim B., Patrick P., Harry S., Michelle W., Kim M., Claire, L., Barbara H., Tosha H., Carmen S., Michael H., Amber S., LaEsposa O., Sarah R., Stacy C., James C., Sue W., Stacie C., Steve D., Kaitlin D., Jan and Jeri N., Patricia W., Barb and Stuart M., Jenny M., Kevin T., Melissa M., Laurie W., Steven W., Aliza M., Kathy C., Christine F., Rafael V., Jessica F., Megan and Tony H., Dana D., Jason A., Bean O., Rebecca H., Crystal G., Anne H., Rachel G., Kathleen R., Andrew M., Sharon S., Joseph Z., Mary C., Maureen S., Sarah and John W., John and Joanne C., Patrick W., Peggy O., Bob and Cynde D., Joshua W., Kevin and Andrea R., The Osborne Family, Fran T., Karen N., AJ F., Tsaka D., Michelle C., Britney S., Alicia D., John and Linda M., Shirley S., Shaun J., Ryan R., Dave S., Loni W., Jason K., Samantha T., John M., Greg P., Pam J., Kathy M., Steven C., Linnea E., Maggie J., Chris A., Alexis S., Veronica F., Martin F., Alma and Morris G., Nicole A., Adrienne O., Nat I., Gillian R., Jerry R., Sheila L., Jennifer, M., Paul D., Jennifer B., Cailtin P., Cindy and David T., Sherry and Al F., Claudia Z., The Simon Family, Nola D., Ms. M, Megan H., Alissa B., Sarah C., Jeff S., Wendra T., Marty S., Lanah D., Martina R., Trevor T., Jacqueline C., Michelle J., Amy M., Brittney J., Karleigh S., Tommy B., Haley and Gary I., Sara H., John M., Darlene and Bill D., Christine L., Carrie C., Mary Jane S., Jason H., Eileen

S., Sarah H., Barbara K., Liz C., The Messina Family, Aaron S., Marcia S., Jeffrey C., Katie T., Martha D., Adam P., Ryan T., Alexandra and Wyatt H., Heather D., Stephanie K., Raymond H., Lisa P., Emily Taddeo., Casey K., Elaine S., Laura V., Jeffrey T., Katherine M., Kelly T., Jeff M., Emily C., Ellie C., Stephanie P., Emily A., Margaret F., Donna L., Jud and Kris M., Jacqueline V., Ellen Z., Thomas H., Laurie R., Jeff B., Laura W., Mike F., Melissa J., Amy L., Joan S., Carrie R., Lori M., Ginny B., Kettia M., Alex O., Frank R., Alison D., Gary L., Jim and Rena N., Valerie M., Tom S., Nora M., Mary Anne and Ralph E., Sue and Todd T., Angela M., Gail W., Linda B., Kristin W., Betty P., Kathy A., Bill and Lori L., Chris D., Sarah L., Scott S., Paula B., Regina F., Susan S., Kelly M., Anne M., Evan R., Kira S., Kelly G., Cindy M., Kirsten L., Pete and Sharon V., Bob C., Mitchell C., Stephen A., Lilah C., Sarah R., Denise G., Bob H., Suzanne A., Jen S., Caroline W., Kyle K., Mallory M., Mary Anne and Mike H., Emma F., Tim K., Renee R., Deb H., Bob C., Kara and Eric N., Margaret C., Meridith W., Whitney A., Mia C., Bev C., Barb H., Mark S., Jeff J., Gail Y., James E., Peter M., Courtney S., Megan W., Donna and Tom H., Jenny M., Michael L., John and Karen F., Alexander O., Pat F., Diana and Jason C., Dan and Dana N., Gail B., Tara D., Michelle S., Tamara T., MaryBeth and Greg P., Carol M., Rachel and Dave G., Martha U., Dorothy D., Roseann M., Jackie B., Sara D., Brittany W., Joanne K., James and Bunni S., Lorraine E., William M., Kathleen O., Nicole B., Gary S., Susan E., Michael E., Jan and Andy R., Melissa R., Jen S., Matthew E., John C., Kara B., Paul and Julie F., Andrew R., Alyson O., Josie J., Tracy H., David V., Matthew H., Scott and Sarah V., Eileen W., Joan and Tom M., Nick M., Constance C., Amy G., Kelly P., Emily G., Christine S., Nancy B., Marguerite P., Hari R., Tom R., Catherine N., Marie and John L., Rachel K., Barbara C., Cliff B., Jen A., Elaine A., Lindsay H., Edward W., Raj B., Sandra W., Lorraine F., Devon M., Dan and Alex P., Andrea C., Jenn H., Michelle D., Brittnye S., Mandy S., Mike and Tamara G., Eleanor S., Leah M., Debra W., Erin K., Rhonda B., Mike V., Randall J., Chad and Kim P., Bryant S., Danielle C.,

Bruce T., Steven L., Jillian D., Heather H., Emily G., Patricia D., Jim V., Ashley E., Colleen C., Matt and Vicky M., Tiffany B., Amy W., Keith P., Joe Z., Ken F., Emily H., Sharon F., Alison M., Joe C., Amy T., Lucas H., Jamie R., Janie G., Jennifer V., Mark and Susan R., Sue and Andy S., Kathleen P., Laura B., LouAnne B., Catie A., The Fello Family, Angie and Mimi L., Shannon T., Johnny R., Brian L., Jenny and Brian O., Jess Q., Alan C., Jessica and Dave S., Richard L., Sara V., Frank G., Vaugh F., Ann F., Stephanie R., Adrianne M., Sarah H., JoAnn W., Shaun A., Tina S., Mary L., Robert P., Kelly O., Matt and Courtney H., Kris S., Christy and Tim M., Wendy H., Jaci J., Jessica, Jason, Ella and Charlotte K., Marc T., Jena F., Kelly U., Rexine and John F., Ruth L., Cara D., Joe and Deb D., Kim S., Eileen H., Michael R., The Parrotts, Laura C., Dana H., Jess and Tim O., Marsha and Jason P., Shelly B., Laurence D., Rebecca G., Angela and Wes B., Will C., Amy M., Kelly S., Gina P., Jacqueline L. Joe C., Sam Z., Nicole S., Bev E., Lindsay and Dave S., Kathryn M., Sarah P., Yvette O., Joy M., Ally T., Chris W., Melissa M., Kevin D., Jen C., Rebecca M., Josh R., Allison W., Julie D., Ishla P., Gordon L., Aaron T., Charles A., Steve M., Stu E., Justina S., Frank H., Maureen S., Crystal A., Kiel H., Daniel D., Justin D., Al and Sunne M., Susie T., Ryan T., Kelly and Michael W., Deanna and Steve C., Morgan B., Kip W., Jason K., Bob and Katie P., Lisa D., Lisa G., Meghan W., Mike and Renee S., Carl and Kelley M., Renee S., Rebecca W., Megan M., Vicky B., Shiloh W., Nikki A., Kristin J., Laura L., Molly M., Meredith B., Chelsea F., Melinda D., Barbara M., Joseph B., Laura S., Jon C., Don and Ann H., Patrick D., Teresa F., Ryan S., Angela D., Kathleen B., Pete P., Nicole R., Michael R., Jeremy Q., Heather G., Cassandra and Emilee M., Susan H., Jim S., Laura F., Laura F., Heather M., Matthew R., Jessica K., Taylor K., Jim C., Kathy M., Adam L., Susan B., Lauren B., Cheryl F., David C., Meghan P., Laura T., Tiffany D., Andrew and Caren D., Ronnika P., Nora H., Anna B., Rob S., Lisa M., Beth Ann S., David M., Stacie P., Robert C., Sarah M., Troy S., Shaun S., Abigail A., Candice A., Richie A., Chris S., Jason R., Angie S., and each and every Anonymous donor.

About Atmosphere Press

Founded in 2015, Atmosphere Press was built on the principles of Honesty, Transparency, Professionalism, Kindness, and Making Your Book Awesome. As an ethical and author-friendly hybrid press, we stay true to that founding mission today.

If you're a reader, enter our giveaway for a free book here:

SCAN TO ENTER
BOOK GIVEAWAY

If you're a writer, submit your manuscript for consideration here:

SCAN TO SUBMIT
MANUSCRIPT

And always feel free to visit Atmosphere Press and our authors online at atmospherepress.com. See you there soon!

ABOUT THE AUTHOR

Courtesy of Sara Rose Photography

SARA LAWLER SMITH is a 40-something nurse who currently resides in Nashville Tennessee via the Finger Lakes Region of New York. While she has no previous publications, she has always had a passion for writing and anything related to the arts. She shares her home with her dogs, sociopathic cat, and husband.

Made in United States
North Haven, CT
27 June 2023

38308676R00136